THE RETURN OF
MERLIN

BY MICHAEL DEAN

GLOBAL COMMUNICATIONS

Editorial Direction & Layout
Timothy Green Beckley

Composition and design:
Cross-Country Consultants
8858 E. Palm Ridge Drive
Scottsdale, AZ 85260

Cover Art by Barbara Lynn

Published by:
GLOBAL COMMUNICATIONS
P.O. Box 753
New Brunswick, NJ 08903

Free catalog of books upon request.

ISBN: 0-938294-30-X

Contents

Introduction by James MacIver Bell   4
Foreword by Sir George Trevelyan   7

2. ENTER THE MAGICIAN

1   The Reappearance of Merlin   10
     "The Archmage"   11
2   We're off to see the Wizard   12
     Merlin speaks   16
3   Links with Space   17
4   Enter the Magician   22

2. THE QUEST GATHERS PACE

5   Merlin keeps his promise   26
6   Birds of a feather   30
     "Look up, look inward…"   32
7   With a little help from our friends   33
     "Human energy…"   37
8   Hidden powers   38
9   A cry from the heart   46
     "Alchemists"   52

3. THE GUARDIANS

10   Friends in high places   54
"   *The constellations of the Zodiac…"*   57
11   Enter the King   58
     "Will, Love/wisdom and Intelligence"   60
12   Enter the Lady   61
     "Seek the Light…"   64
13   Enter the Master of Ceremonies   65
14   Another promise fulfilled   70

4. OPERATION EXCALIBUR

15   The Circle of Light   77
     "Adjustments must now be made…"   83
16   A midsummer moment   84
17   Into the field   86
     "The current model of a man…"   90
18   The Circle of Power   91

19   Operation Excalibur   95
20   Manittoo!   97
21   Overture to a new Age   100
22   Squaring those corn circles   102
23   Things to come?   105

5. INITIATIONS

24   Facets of myself   110
25   Gifts from the Mage   112
26   Into the Sun   115
27   Return to Avalon   120
28   The chalice   127
     "Across the celestial ocean…"   129

6. TOWARDS THE GRAIL

20   Just for the record   131
30   Merlin, Arthur and the Holy Grail   137
31   Mission: Earth   140
32   A blueprint for the future   144
     "That mysterious force…"   149
33   Time to wake up   150
     "The long, dark night is over…"   152
34   Dear friend, take heart   153
35   Last chance   155
     "Look to your children…"   158
36   Exit the Wizard   159
37   The path to the Grail   161
     "Only one starship…"   164
38   The never-ending story   165
39   Across the horizon in overdrive   176
40   Dear Ava   179
41   The Ceremony   182

7. FULL CIRCLE

42   A bolt from beyond   186
43   Full Circle   150
44   The Wind of Change   195
45   Dream   200
46   Making mastic   206
47   State of the Nation   213
48   The Hopi Prophecy   215
     Companions   222
     Curtain Call   228
     Index   232

"I read this lovely book straight away—no reason to stop once I'd started—and was carried right through to the end by the tidal wave of anecdotes, sketches, scenes and insights on which the author sweeps through it. A great delight, and just what these times are like.

"Yes, we do live in a wonderful world, regaining our natural right to angels, coincidences and miracles. How blind we have been! What revelations are abroad! He has hit just the right note and sustained it all through. I just wish Tony Roberts [author of *Atlantean Traditions in Ancient Britain*] had lived to see this: he would have reveled."

John Michell
Author of *The View Over Atlantis*
and *City of Revelation*

"The return of the angels to human consciousness could be one of the greatest surprises of the twentieth century..."

H C Moolenburgh, MD
A Handbook of Angels [C W Daniel]

INTRODUCTION

The huge success of the movies *Close Encounters of the Third Kind* and *ET, the Extraterrestrial* suggests that a vast number of people around the world not only identify with the idea of help coming from "out there", but that they are positively yearning for it.

This could be interpreted in the following way:

For the first time in recorded history, mankind as a whole —or a sizeable proportion of it, regardless of race, culture and religion—is calling for help.

Why should this be?

Because, alongside our creative genius and ingenuity in so many fields, there is in us a cruel and destructive streak which spawned the technology that has now brought us all to the very brink of self-annihilation.

The painful truth is dawning on us that this crisis does not lie "over there" in so-called enemy territory, or somewhere in the Third World, but right here in our own back yard. In fact it lies inside each and every one of us, and its outcome depends directly on our finding the courage to face the darker side of our nature. Then and only then are we likely to admit that many of our current institutions are corrupt and no longer workable, and that drastic solutions must now be found.

In other words, we have learned the hard way that whatever you and I do affects everyone else on Earth, and that whatever everyone else does affects you and me. Like it or not, we are all in this thing together.

Now *Close Encounters* and *ET* struck a resonant chord within millions of us; their imagery was powerful and appealing, they were brilliantly constructed. But what did we actually learn from these visitors from Space? We caught a glimpse of timelessness and high technology from the former, a taste of magic and childlike humour from the latter; little else. It was as if we had been led into a glittering banquet hall—but the

4

moment we reached for the wine and the food, they crumbled to dust in our mouths, leaving a haunting memory of their splendour and the pangs of unappeased hunger.

Here, then, is some very good news:

Not a flying saucer or mother ship; not a spaceman from somewhere out there in the galaxy; but a number of radiant beings from a higher Universe—and one in particular who once, long ago, appeared in human guise and has lingered in our memory ever since. Clearly, he is as deeply concerned with us and our struggles as he ever was; so much so that in recent years he has been contacting an ever-increasing number of people on both sides of the Atlantic.

His name?

Merlin. And it has become all too obvious to his many contactees that the name "Merlin" and his wizard's guise are only one tiny facet of a cosmic being of limitless creativity and intelligence.

In 1974, Merlin asked Michael Dean if he could share with him certain information "which might throw light not only on your own life, and the work you and your companions are doing, but also on the distant past, on this crucial planetary moment, and on the future."

Deeply impressed by the benign, majestic presence of the Magician and his ripe sense of humour, Michael was only too glad to accept the offer—or "summons", as he prefers to call it. And so began an extraordinary adventure that is still gathering momentum.

One of Merlin's primary aims was to present a picture of our world and our place in it that is simple, encouraging and crystal clear. Another was to urge those who heard his voice to discard centuries of dogma, misinformation and systems that have outlived their usefulness. A third tactic was to feed in a series of clues or pieces of key information which Michael and his friends slowly began to assemble into a gigantic jigsaw puzzle.

This book, which offers intriguing glimpses of their quest, echoes a long and time-honoured tradition: in the past, whenever the human race has got itself into trouble, help has arrived from exalted sources. Either some ascended being has taken on human form and lived among us long enough to share his or her wisdom with us, or has miraculously appeared to someone and left a vital message, warning or promise. The world's sacred literature is littered with instances of these attempts to shed light on our path.

But then what happens? We bury these beings and their message in every kind of ritual and orthodoxy, and end up with a handful of major religions, each claiming—despite the fact that the same light burns at the heart of them all—that it is the Only Way. As a result, we have had to endure centuries of unholy wars. The carnage is continuing this very day.

Merlin urges us, whatever our beliefs, to look for the spirit or essence *behind* everything, and not to become enslaved to its outward form. He even begs us to reject anything *he* says that does not seem right to us. The very last thing he would wish is for anyone to build a cult around him and the guidance he offers.

He simply states that, if we can think for *ourselves*, develop ourselves—*and allow others to do likewise*—our perspectives will automatically widen and our sympathy and understanding will grow large enough to embrace all people and all forms of life. That done, we can begin to climb, at last, out of the traps we have dug for ourselves and into the light of a brilliant new century.

James MacIver Bell

FOREWORD

Who and what is Merlin? What is this magic and mystery? It seems that there is in so many people an irrepressible hope that this is real: that Arthur, the Once and Future King, is coming again and that he represents a Kingdom which will bring a flood of divine warmth and light into our embattled world. And Merlin, his magician, is the power which oversees and inspires us as we approach the point of no return.

We are all touched by this impulse, this light, this love, which melts the rigidity of frozen hardness and allows a flow of living energy, bringing the warmth of a new spring.

No question but that it is *real*. The change is taking place, a redemption of the dying Age by an inflooding of the light frequency of limitless Love and Truth. This creates a living magnetic field around any body which consciously attunes. Thus it gives complete protection against negative influence by surrounding a person, a group, a centre, even a country, with a radiating field of life and harmony. But it clearly needs human initiative to set this process into effective action, since humanity has been given a freedom which the angelic worlds will always respect.

Now Merlin is the magician, guardian and mentor to Arthur the King, who is regent to Michael, sword-bearer of the Cosmic Kings. Here is the gradation of command in this operation for the redemption of the material world.

The "wild hope" of the coming again of Merlin and Arthur, obstinately held somewhere in our consciousness, represents this impulse, which is a truth. In our age, an energy which is Life/Light/Love floods the Earth, re-animating the realm of matter:

"And thus corruption shall put on incorruption and this mortal shall put on immortality and we shall all be changed..."

Crisis and cataclysm in our time mean opportunity and transformation. And if we could really be surrounded by this forcefield of Divine magnetic power, we would have complete protection—perhaps the *only* protection we would ever need—to enable us to grow to fulfillment.

This remarkable book is an expression of this sublime hope in our age of turmoil.

Sir George Trevelyan, Bt.

1. ENTER THE MAGICIAN

1 THE REAPPEARANCE OF MERLIN

"If you were to study a map of England and plot on it some of the power centres that are already known, you would find a design emerging, and from this design you can begin to build a picture that reflects the evolution of the Earth itself.

"The power waiting to be tapped at these sources—by those of you with unselfish motives, and this I cannot overstress—could generate peace and confidence among the people of the world, thereby adding impetus to the forces of Light in this ever-intensifying battle between harmony and chaos.

"The time is coming fast when Merlin will awake, and once more these power centres will be revitalised and made available to those who know the secret of extracting the sword Excalibur. It will be up to groups like your own to look into the harnessing of these powers for the benefit of mankind."

This remarkable prophecy was made in January 1967 by Helio-Arcanophus, an angelic being who, since the mid-1950s, has been helping groups throughout Britain to relate "the Ancient Wisdom" to our lives today, and shedding light on our troubled relationship with Nature and all forms of life. Seven years later, in the spring, H-A's prophecy came true—for me, at least. I had a vivid dream, in which I was looking down at a landscape dominated by two hills or mountains that rose to needle-sharp peaks, forming a gigantic capital "M". A good friend, John Prudhoe, appeared quietly at my side and said: "I am to take you to see the Magician."

Immediately the scene changed and I was standing with John in a small anteroom. At the far end stood a tall, heavily-built man with long flowing hair and a beard, pale in colour. Unsmiling, he beckoned me forward. Rather nervously, I advanced. He took my right hand and briefly examined the palm. On it we both saw a cross contained by a circle. The Magician's face lit up in a huge smile. He flung his arms wide and clasped me to his massive frame in a welcoming bear-hug.

My adventures with Merlin were about to begin.

"Merlin, the Archmage. A great arche-typal symbol of the man who, by deduc-tion, has extended his perception successfully beyond the consciousness of the five senses and mere reason. He served and guided Arthur in the affairs of his Kingdom, teaching the young man to work with the soul senses guided by intu-ition. He was a very great influence in Atlantean days, and even earlier. The Islands of Britain are known to some as *'Merlin's Enclosure'*."

Debbie Rice
Guarding Merlin's Enclosure

2 WE'RE OFF TO SEE THE WIZARD

Midsummer day, 1974. The sky bluer than blue. Our little convoy of two cars sped through the flatlands south of Glastonbury—water-meadows, ancient hedges, mossed apple orchards, a sense of timelessness—towards our destination, Park Wood.

We slowed at an intersection where a number of small houses, not even a hamlet, basked in the warmth of early afternoon. From behind his garden gate, a red-faced farmer in brown tweed trousers and a collarless shirt watched us approach. He might almost have been waiting for us.

We pulled up. Tony, the lead driver, leaned out of his window.

"Park Wood?"

The farmer took in the two cars and their occupants. The red face reddened still further.

"Bloody hippies. How did *you* get a Volvo Estate, then?"

He didn't actually say it. He didn't need to—his face said it for him.

Tony smiled, tried again:

"Is that Park Wood?" He indicated a dark wall of trees on the skyline, a mile or so to our left.

"That's private land," the farmer snapped. "You can't—"

"Duke of Edinburgh's Wildfowl Scheme," I cut in, flourishing a reporter's notebook in my window. "Drive on."

Biting back a grin, Tony did so. Our convoy rolled on, and within two minutes we had parked on the grass verge overlooking a small, compact, almost circular wood.

This must be it.

We climbed out, stretched our legs, locked the cars.

There were eight of us including Tony and Silver's little daughter, Layla. We trudged across a field to the perimeter of the wood, and halted. More hostility: a taut four-strand barbed-wire fence, in good condition. Stoically we shrugged our shoulders, determined not to be put off.

With some difficulty we surmounted this barrier—Silver and Layla squeezing between the bottom two rows of barbed wire which Tony and Simon held open for them—and began to make our way through shoulder-high grass, nettles and brambles towards the heart of the wood: a single-file safari of townies, mystics and explorers.

Layla, riding on Tony's shoulders, started to grizzle. We hacked and muttered, giggled and swore, several times coming to a full stop in the dense, almost impenetrable undergrowth.

A brief eternity later, we erupted onto a track running clear through the wood. A wide track. Not exactly the Yellow Brick Road, but if I tell you that two combine harvesters going in opposite directions could have passed each other on it with room to spare, you'll get the general idea.

We burst out laughing, brushed the burrs and thistles off our clothes, flicked seeds and dead grass from our hair, nursed assorted stings and scratches. It occurs to me now—it didn't then—that Silver and Layla were Dorothy; Tony, with his love of machines, motors and all things mechanical, must have been our Tin Man; gangling Simon, all six foot three of him, the Straw Man; and I, presumably, a well-meaning but none-too-efficient Leo, must have been the Lion. The only one missing was Toto. He would have tunnelled through the undergrowth and got here long before us.

The farmer? He was probably one of the henchmen serving the Wicked Witch of the West—put in our path to try to stop us reaching our destination.

"Brilliant," said Simon sarcastically.

"Yeah," I agreed. "Terrific fieldcraft. Sorry about that."

An hour later, we discovered that if we'd spent just one minute examining the perimeter fence, we could have walked into the wood along this track, eight abreast if we'd wanted to. It has since struck me that our cack-handed, heavy-footed arrival in Park Wood was a classic example of our knack of doing things the hard way; of being so intent on the drama or glamour of the quest that we miss what's under our noses all the time.

We decided to split up, and agreed to meet back on the track in half an hour, to exchange reports.

I found myself in a little sunlit glade—slender birches in

an approximate circle, knee-high grass, occasional wild-flowers; midges dancing through the still air. The silence was absolute.

I closed my eyes and tried to still my mind. I wondered if this expedition was going to turn out to be a wild goose chase after all. Our entry into the ancient wood already had all the elements of farce.

Why were we here—trespassing, probably—in the heart of a small Somerset wood?

Three reasons:

First, one of England's greatest seers had said that the ancient ground-plan we now call the Glastonbury Zodiac "was designed to attract and blend rays from the constellations above and from the Masters there who are the embodiment of divinity in other planets throughout the Universe." One of the first recorded references to this Zodiac—in which, as you probably know, the symbols of all twelve constellations have been "drawn" on the land, using roads, hedges and other natural features—was made by Dr John Dee, magician and adviser to Queen Elizabeth I. He called it "Merlin's Secret".

Secondly, it is believed in certain circles that this masterwork was created thousands of years ago by scouts from Atlantis who, knowing that their civilisation was about to end, sought a safe new home for some of their knowledge, which they hoped would be rediscovered in time to come.

And thirdly, a week or so before our expedition, I had been re-reading Anthony Roberts' *Atlantean Traditions in Ancient Britain* and came across these words:

"...the exact centre point of this Zodiac is found at tiny Park Wood on the outskirts of the village of Butleigh. It is here if anywhere that the last of the Druid Magicians, Merlinus Albionis [Merlin], would have left his body when he departed the confines of this world in 500 A.D. It is beneath the brown soil of Park Wood that the new seekers of his ornate stone sarcophagus may one day unearth a miracle. The long slumber of Blake's 'Giant Albion' is now drawing to a close, and the revelation of new life is rising like the first stirrings of a late spring..."

I can't explain it, but those words seemed to be an invitation. A summons, almost. Right then and there, I knew something was going to come of it...

Without warning, a voice broke the silence in the little glade where I now stood, deep in thought:

"Do not seek Excalibur on the physical plane. The places where we worked still carry our vibrations, but over the centuries the true power has been stored and guarded on the inner planes. Only when groups like yours are attuned to the highest pitch will you be able to unlock some of the power that is still available—for correct use."

I stood rooted to the spot, my heart pounding. A flush of excitement rose to my cheeks. The voice was as clear as if someone had spoken beside me.

But it had come from inside my own head.

It was the Magician himself, of that I am convinced. Some things just *are*, and that voice had been Merlin's. Not the deep, resonant voice I was to encounter some months later, when the Wizard spoke through someone who is about to enter this story and play a leading role in it; but a voice as clear as crystal, with no traceable accent or dialect.

I hurried back to my companions, blithely unaware of the train of events that had just been set in motion, and where it was going to lead in years to come...

MERLIN SPEAKS

"For long ages we have been working towards a period when our powers will be taxed to the utmost. It should come as no surprise, therefore, to learn that this period is now upon us.

"Many drastic changes have taken place in your world during the last one hundred and fifty years—not all of them for the better. As man's material conditions have improved, his spiritual life has atrophied and he has lost sight of the debt he owes the planet which sustains him, and the many unseen intelligences who work unceasingly on behalf of the human race.

"Starship Earth has been pilotless far too long. Indeed, some of your fellow crew members have forgotten so much about the direction and ultimate purpose of your flight that they are plundering the ship's stores in an orgy of self-indulgence.

"It is your individual duty to re-attune to the craft that is carrying you, to restore the sight of your fellows if you can. The Earth will soon pass on to your children. Learn from *them*. Teach them to cherish their mother ship, and acquaint them with some of *her* needs.

"Become aware of the subtle energies flowing within, through and around you; tune in to the energies that permeate the planet herself. Rediscover the wisdom that your distant ancestors once attained; blend with it the highest achievements of today. This alchemy alone will put your starship back on course, when once again it can resume its proper journey."

Hertfordshire, 1975

16

3 LINKS WITH SPACE

A few weeks after our visit to Park Wood, I finished writing a novel, *Catch The Lightning,* about a woman with special powers who is employed by British Intelligence to protect a visiting American envoy, sent by the President on a delicate diplomatic mission. She helps to foil an attempt on his life, and before he returns to Washington he asks her to put on tape a summary of where she's coming from, as he feels it might be important. Rather reluctantly, she agrees to do so.

So *I* had to produce the tape. How the hell do you give someone your perspective on "the Universe and life and everything" in four minutes?! I went out into Regent's Park, sat on my favourite seat in a secluded garden, took out pen and paper, looked up at the sky and said, "Okay, Merlin, ready when you are!"

Within seconds, my pen was flying across the page.

"Hey, hold on a sec—you know I don't have shorthand!"

And from that day on, whenever I came to a particularly crucial or difficult scene in a screenplay or whatever, I always put out a call. And was always answered.

This doesn't mean I no longer have to do anything difficult—I'm offered help, but *I* have to do the work of interpreting it as best I can. More often than not, it takes four or five drafts before the result is anywhere near usable. In movie-making, the ratio between film shot and film finally used can be as high as 15 to 1. Well, it's about the same with me—for every fifteen pages I sling into the wastepaper basket, I'm lucky if I end up with one usable page.

Anyway, on this particular occasion, it was all over in minutes—and needed almost no editing later. I took the transcript, *Links With Space,* to my friend Peter Carbines, our brilliant sound engineer, and he put together some music and effects for it.

Next midsummer, despite the expected local opposition, a free festival was held in Windsor Great Park. Moments before sunset, a rather ragged and under-rehearsed band finished their

17

set, leaving the crowd camped out on the hillside restless and disorientated.

Tony, who was in charge of the PA, decided that this was the moment to lay *Links* on an audience, and inserted the tape. We all heard a colossal galactic explosion, underscored by an elusive, almost subliminal music track. As the sound slowly faded, the commentary began:

> "There was always It, or God, the Ultimate—timeless, formless. It decided to convert some of its potential into form, and to let individuality express itself at every level...

> "The Universes were the result, all of them links in an endless cosmic chain...

> "At the lower end of this chain is the physical Universe, crystallised in time and space. Its many worlds are living beings, who act as hosts to other forms of life...

> "We ourselves come from a higher Universe. We visit Earth many times, to experience physical life in all its aspects, and at the end of each lifetime we return to the inner worlds...

> "The truth lies hidden within and around us all; each of us must dig for our share of this buried treasure. And yet free will allows us to live in light or darkness, as we choose...

> "Everything we do, returns to us sooner or later. This is Law, and never varies. As individuals, families and nations, we cre-

ate our own destiny—no-one else does...

"The Earth has been described as a kidney in the body of the Solar System, designed to filter and transmute impurities. It is also known to some as the planet of healing and music...

"All energies are neutral. We can use them to create or destroy. Our misuse of the atom is causing havoc on several levels beyond our own...

"Surrounding the Earth like a layer of cloud are all our darker thoughts and feelings. If we can disperse this cloud, we'll see that we're all lights in the same circuit, and the power that drives it is Love...

"The present chapter in world history is about to end, and another to begin. It'll be a brighter chapter, demanding all our effort and resources. Already, mankind is awakening to the challenge...

"At last we'll start swimming *with* the currents in the galaxy, rather than against them. We'll be playing a more positive role in the great experiment called Life...

"Having rediscovered our real identity, we'll begin to respect ourselves, each other and all forms of life; to serve our community, to love and protect our starship/mother, Earth...

"Our minds will reach out into the Solar System and beyond. We'll be exploring frequencies higher than the physical. Once we tune in to them, we can enjoy two-way traffic with these worlds and their inhabitants—who include everyone who has ever lived and 'died' on Earth. No-one and nothing is ever lost...

"Everything that has ever happened in this world is imprinted on the ether. These etheric records unfold like a never-ending motion picture. Eventually all life forms, worlds, systems and galaxies will return to It, or God, the Ultimate—timeless, formless...

"The capital 'U' in Universe tells us the story: like the curve on the graph of our journey, it first shows our descent into matter, then a period of comparative horizontality, and finally a climb back to the Source...

"Around us are all the clues we need to lift us out of the quicksands of space and time, and to set our feet on the upward path that will lead us all back home."

Like a galaxy wheeling slowly away down the long, dark corridors of Space, the music died away to utter silence.

For a full fifteen seconds, nobody in the crowd moved. At that precise moment, the sun dipped behind the horizon.

A day or so later, a friend phoned Tony to thank him for all the work he had put into the festival.

"...and you know that tape you played on the last night, at sunset? Did you see what happened as it ended?"

20

"No. What?" said Tony.

"You didn't *see* it?! A UFO appeared high above the PA, hovered for a few moments, then sped away at incredible speed…"

4 ENTER THE MAGICIAN

During November of the same year, a novel that Robert Donaldson and I had written—it is called *Wilderness,* and is the story of a mysterious American living alone in the remote rain-forests of northern Australia—was released. Our publisher arranged for me to guest on Adrian Love's LBC late-night chat show.

I asked Adrian if he would play *Links With Space* for openers. Without even asking what it was, Adrian said, "Sure, why not?" So that night, a quarter of a million Londoners found themselves on an unscheduled flight! When the tape came to an end, Adrian swallowed hard, grinned, and cued a commercial break, "So I can get my breath back..."

For the next two and a half hours, between records—for some reason I was his only guest that night—Adrian and I talked about the consciousness explosion that was occurring throughout the western world, the resurgence of interest in so-called paranormal phenomena and personal transformation.

Enthusiastic listeners phoned in, and those two and a half hours sped by in what seemed like minutes.

Several letters came in during the following week, and by far the most interesting was from a film cameraman, Peter Quiller, in Hertfordshire. We clearly had several interests in common, and an almost identical sense of humour. We struck up an immediate correspondence which would soon develop into friendship.

Peter had been investigating psychic phenomena, recording the sound in haunted churches, attending a development circle and the like, but had already become rather disenchanted with such things—his description of the posturing and preening that went on in that circle was to have me doubled up with laughter, when we finally met—and now wrote to tell me that he felt he was "on the threshold of something much bigger."

As he was clearly about to move up an octave, as it were, I encouraged him to concentrate on his own inner development and to let go the other stuff which, as his wife Bran rightly said, had merely been a series of preliminary steps along the way.

Pete did so. And three months later, it happened. In a letter, he takes up the story:

"I woke at about three o'clock in the morning. The bed felt as if it was swinging from side to side, my head felt light and I sensed that I could have floated quite easily out of the window. It was a mid-March night, within a week of the Equinox. There, in the middle of the bedroom, floated a wide band of purple energy reaching from floor to ceiling. Within it shone a myriad gold and silver pinpoints of light that swirled about like constellations in miniature. I estimated that the purple column was at least eight feet across; top and bottom seemed to disappear into the ceiling and floor…

"Suddenly a beam of light shot towards me and hit me straight between the eyes. There was a blinding flash. 'I'm dead,' I thought. 'It's killed me!' But I immediately felt at peace.

"And then a disembodied voice, coming from the purple column, began to speak, assuring me that I had nothing to fear—and adding that we had worked together many times! I kept trying to wake Bran, but she was fast asleep and didn't budge. For several minutes the voice continued, then announced, 'And now I must leave you.'

" 'But who the hell *are* you?' I asked, rather bluntly.

" 'What's in a name?' it replied. 'I have been known by many, many names. You may call me Merlin. Welcome home, my son… Welcome home.' "

Pete then heard the sound of "rich, resonant laughter which slowly faded away in a procession of echoes." Stunned and exhausted, he fell asleep, "curiously at ease with the concept of meeting *him* again…"

A while later, Pete invited me to visit him and Bran at their Hertfordshire cottage, as "M" wished to speak to me. It was an unforgettable meeting. Pete and Bran were "family" from the word go—no breaking the ice, no testing the water were necessary: it was as if we already knew each other, and had done so for years.

Pete had long brown hair that tumbled to his shoulders, a full beard and the girth of a young Falstaff. His laugh rattled the window-frames. Bran, buxom, vivacious and attractive, had a natural Welsh wisdom and, like Pete, an earthy sense of humour.

After supper, when the children had gone to bed, Pete lowered the lights in the little sitting room and prepared himself. Bran sat nearby.

Slowly the darkened room filled with an indescribable energy, deep purple and humming like a power station, then Pete was overshadowed by this awesome presence. I felt as if I was standing at the foot of a huge, benevolent mountain. The voice, appropriately enough, rolled down like thunder from its upper slopes.

It was Merlin.

He opened his arms in welcome and—just like the Magician in my recent dream—clasped me to him in a bear-like embrace. No possible doubt about it, I decided as the minutes passed, this was the Merlin all right—the combination of majesty, intelligence, power and compassion; the occasional roar of despair at human folly and perversity and, above all, the earthquakes of laughter could only be the great Archmage himself…

I went home the next evening, my head buzzing with memories of this momentous reunion. ["Yes, reunion—not first encounter," 'M' had insisted.] I undressed, turned out the lights and went to bed.

A moment or two later, I sensed brilliant light in the room. I opened my eyes. For another three seconds the room was ablaze with dazzling white light. Then it went out. There had been no sound whatsoever.

I lay in the dark, my heart pounding, trying to find a reasonable explanation for what had just happened. Eventually I fell asleep.

I could hardly wait to visit Pete again. He brought Merlin through as before, and at the end of our conversation—which ranged over a number of topics, including current world affairs, the future, and the likelihood of geophysical changes on Earth within our lifetime—I told "M" about the light in my room, and asked if he knew what it had been.

"Me," was his terse, amused reply.

2. THE QUEST GATHERS PACE

5 MERLIN KEEPS HIS PROMISE

In the years that followed, Merlin was to become an indispensable guide, tutor and friend. He showed himself in many guises, but the overriding impression we received was of an energy rather than a person, an energy that had its origin outside the stellar Universe altogether. And yet there was nothing remote or impersonal about him or his communications—which we soon came to recognise by their unique blend of compassion and dispassion, utter candour and uproarious good humour.

For all that, he was extremely outspoken on the subject of man's outrageous attitude to women and his treatment of them; and equally scathing about our callous abuse of "your mother, Earth, who, uncomplaining, supplies your every need."

He several times urged us to treat him as an equal, as we would an elder brother, and not to hold him in awe:

"You do not always have to agree with me," he would say. "Truth is a many-splendoured thing; have opinions of your *own*."

In June 1977 he said to me, "I shall prepare an objective vision for your eyes alone. Be prepared..."

A week or two later, Tony, Silver, Petey and I drove to Glastonbury. Before climbing the Tor, we visited Chalice Well garden and drank water from the ancient well—crystal clear, iron-tinged, delicious. It was hot, so we sprawled on the small lawn for a while in silence.

I was lying on my back, shielding my eyes from the sun, when a small mottled bird flew into my field of vision and began to hover directly above me at about forty feet.

A Merlin hawk.

The first shock hit my solar plexus: it was the exact shape of a Spitfire!

Then a second shock: the Spitfire was powered by the Merlin engine! And played a vital part in saving Britain in 1940. For a moment I lay there, transfixed, unable to speak or move.

The hawk, having delivered its message, dipped its wings and flew off over Chalice Hill.

As soon as I could, I visited Pete and asked Merlin if he

had inspired Mitchell to design the Spitfire during Britain's "darkest hour", and also Sir Henry Royce and his engineers who built the Merlin engine.

He chuckled and, in that deep unmistakable voice, replied:

"Why do you ask questions whose answers you already know?!"

It was the most benevolent reprimand you could ever wish to hear.

I decided there and then that to go on thinking of Merlin as some kind of sorcerer or Archdruid would be to miss the point completely. Peter and I had already come to the conclusion that he must be a member of a group of Initiates whose prime function here is to act as agents of change, by drawing our attention to patterns and thought-forms that have outlived their usefulness, and by preparing us for the new energies—however disconcerting they might be—that must replace them.

Whatever else might be said of him, and however limited our perception of his real identity and aims, of one thing we were already convinced:

Merlin had returned—if ever he left—to encourage us, at this crucial planetary moment, in our quest for stability, enlightenment, and survival.

That night, before he left us, the Magician laid his fingertips on my brow and held them there for a while. Next morning, Pete said, "You realise 'M' gave you a gift last night?"

"What kind of a gift?" I asked.

Pete smiled enigmatically. "You'll find out soon enough," he said, and let the matter drop.

In the days that followed, these four incidents occurred—among many others of a similar nature. I think they might have something to do with Merlin's parting gift:

One afternoon of scudding grey cloud and fitful sunshine, so typical of Glastonbury, Tony, Silver and I climbed the Tor to do our usual Solstice number. As we approached the ruined tower on its summit, I said I hoped someone else was up there, so there would be four of us.

There was: just one person—a young American in a dark blue duffel coat, reading a paperback at the foot of the tower. We invited him to join us in our brief meditation, and he seemed glad to be asked.

We went inside, listened to the wind funnelling through the open shaft of the tower, then concentrated deeply.

An impulse made me open my eyes. I studied the American for a moment, and something came into my mind with absolute clarity.

When we had finished, I looked at him again and said, "Steve is very important to you, isn't he?"

Our new companion gazed at me in astonishment, but said nothing.

"He is, isn't he?" I repeated. "Steve."

He nodded. "Yeah, he's my chiropractor back in the States. He fixed my back for me—I used to have a lot of trouble with it. He said I should come to Glastonbury and find out a few things..."

One morning I called on my friend Ronan in Chelsea. A maverick and visionary, with a mane of prematurely white hair—which he probably owes to all the battles he has fought single-handedly against the authorities—and possessed of almost indecent amounts of Irish charm and Irish luck, Ronan had invaded Britain and western Europe with a pair of "pirate" ships in 1964, and overnight *Radio Caroline* relegated the BBC's popular music channel to the Stone Age—and changed the face of popular broadcasting forever.

As I entered his apartment, Ronan introduced me to a young friend of his, Bill, who was fixing a mirror to the wall at the end of the corridor. Bill half-turned, nodded at me and went on working.

I approached him.

"It's Linda for you, isn't it?"

Bill frowned at me in disbelief. "Yes, she's my girl-friend. We're going on holiday to Spain next week."

I had never met Bill or Linda, nor had Ronan ever mentioned them to me before...

Nicolette is a very special friend—one of those rare people you feel you have known for lifetimes. We often don't see each other for years at a stretch, yet every time we meet, we carry on as if it had only been yesterday.

On this occasion she had just returned from India, where she had been painting, and invited me to lunch at her small Kensington apartment. We exchanged progress reports, then she turned to go into the kitchen to prepare our meal.

I "saw" something at her heels.

"There's a small fawn-coloured cat by your feet. Does that make any sense?"

Nicolette smiled. "I certainly does..." While living in Tangier, she had found a starving fawn kitten in a discarded paper bag and nursed it back to health. It became her inseparable companion until its death, shortly before she returned to London...

Petey and I [not Peter Quiller—my group is crawling with Peters!] were having lunch in my small London apartment, talking and laughing in the usual way, when I suddenly stopped, looking round him rather than at him.

"You've got a new girl-friend. Quite unlike the last one. She's dark, plumpish, vivacious, positive, and knows her own mind."

Petey blushed. "Yes," he said after a moment or two. "And her name is..."

If these incidents are indeed part of Merlin's gift, then I thank him. I also thank goodness the process only works occasionally, when *it* wants to, and not on command.

6 BIRDS OF A FEATHER

Another incident that has all the hallmarks of Merlin on it occurred as the summer of 1976 gave way to early autumn:

Almost every afternoon I went out into Regent's Park to feed the birds just beyond the lakeside bandstand. They soon grew so accustomed to me standing with my arms outstretched, like some kind of crazy mobile nut-and-raisin tree, that I could call them out species by species. [I loved the robins most, then the bluetits, then the thrushes, blackbirds, chaffinches—and finally the sparrows who, to say the least, are a bit lacking in the social niceties department.] Only the wrens and dunnocks were too shy to join in the party, so I had to feed them one by one, by stealth.

One day John Prudhoe came to lunch, and over coffee I told him about this feeding ritual. His wry smile told me I was exaggerating.

"Okay, come on, let's go to the park," I said—hoping my customers wouldn't let me down.

We took up our positions, some twenty yards from the railings, and in no time the birds were noisily lining up in the bushes and trees.

Half a dozen sparrows threw caution to the wind and hurtled towards me.

"Later! Your turn comes later!" I yelled, and they returned to the bushes, unabashed.

"That's better." I filled both hands with nuts and raisins and held them out at arm's length.

"Right. Robins!"

Three robins darted out and landed on my hands. When they'd finished eating, they sped back to the bushes.

"Bluetits!"

The same.

"Thrushes!"

Ditto.

"Blackbirds!"

And so on, until only the sparrows remained. I refilled my

hands.

"Okay, you hooligans!"

Within seconds there were at least a dozen sparrows perched on my hands, a dozen more queuing impatiently along my arms and several more flying around jockeying for position.

When it was over, I told John I wanted him to meet a very special friend of mine. We crossed into the inner circle and stopped halfway down a path leading to the park gates.

I broke a peanut into small pieces and held out my hand. "Robin!"

My friend darted out of a nearby tree, landed on my hand and began to eat. When he'd finished, he looked up.

"Would you sing a little song for John and me?" I asked, hoping I wasn't pushing my luck. A number of tourists had gathered near us, and were quietly watching.

The robin sang to us for a while, then stopped.

"Thank you," I said. "That was terrific."

With a whir of wings, the robin flew *round our heads* and back to his tree. John and I exchanged glances, then wordlessly made our way to the rose gardens.

"Surrounded as you are by helpers from every kingdom and from many dimensions, you still insist on walking alone, eyes downcast, in self-imposed exile. Look up, look inward, and your exile, your loneliness will be at an end."

"M"

7 WITH A LITTLE HELP FROM OUR FRIENDS

Merlin's reappearance was living proof to my group that we *are* surrounded by far more unseen friends than we are aware of. The following incident is a powerful and—to me—persuasive illustration of the fact. It was related to Petey and me in her delightful Sussex garden by Kaye Challoner, whose books *The Wheel of Rebirth* and *Regents of the Seven Spheres* are both classics of their kind.

We were privileged to meet this lady during the late 1970s. Almost the twin of Margaret Rutherford, with her perfect enunciation, no-nonsense tweeds and crisp manner, [I wonder if Noël Coward based Madame Arcati in *Blithe Spirit* on her!] she was one of a small band of English mystics—David Anrias and Cyril Scott among them—who had valiantly tended the flame during the 1930s and '40s, when bridge-building between the worlds was a lonely and often derided occupation.

"In the late summer of 1938, I was walking with the Colonel along Camber Sands, on the Sussex coast. Now although he was far too polite to say so, I knew that the Colonel didn't believe in my work and, if pressed, would have called healing, clairvoyance and all the inner work 'claptrap'.

"Suddenly he stopped in his tracks and gazed out over the Channel, towards France. He was frowning.

" 'They're at it again,' he said at last.

" 'Who's at what again?' I asked.

"He shook his head slowly. 'I can only describe them as... as giant beings, and they're building a white wall or curtain between these islands and the mainland of Europe.'

"I laughed inwardly. *This* from an old boy who poo-poohed the spiritual stuff! I don't have to remind you that, against all the odds and probabilities, England was *not* invaded during the War that was about to break out.

"Clever, aren't they, our dear friends 'upstairs'. If *I'd* seen those wall-builders and told the Colonel, he'd have thought I was off my rocker. But *he* saw them...!"

Angelic intervention during wars is far from unknown, especially if our unseen friends consider the cause to be a just one. In his remarkable book *A Handbook of Angels*, Dr H C Moolenburgh tells us of the two following instances, both fully recorded:

During World War I the German army, having just launched a murderous artillery bombardment on the British lines, advanced towards the British trenches south-east of Lille. The defending soldiers, about to be overrun, saw something extraordinary happen:

One minute there was the deafening roar of exploding artillery shells, then they saw the oncoming German troops in their hundreds. The next moment, the barrage stopped and the German infantry had turned tail and were fleeing in disorder.

The British counter-attacked, and took a number of Germans prisoner. These men had an incredible tale to tell: as they were advancing under artillery cover, they suddenly saw a white-clad cavalry regiment mounted on white horses looming up in front of the British lines. At first they thought Moroccan troops must have come to the assistance of the British, so they opened fire on the advancing horsemen with cannon, machine-gun and rifle.

Not a man or horse fell.

And leading the charge was a tall figure with gold hair and a halo round his head.

The Germans panicked, turned tail and retreated with all speed. Strangely enough, the British soldiers hadn't even seen their mysterious protectors...

And late one afternoon in November 1939, a Russian armoured division surrounded an isolated Finnish unit. The Finns prayed for help, and in the night they saw a gigantic angel with outstretched wings appear above their beleaguered garrison. Next morning the Russian division, *unable to find the Finns*, turned and rolled away, seeking other prey. "The Finnish Angel" has now entered into folklore and legend...

And how about this one? A friend of mine at prep school, Lucas, told me that one morning his grandfather, a company commander in France during the 1914—'18 War, received a letter from his wife, Violet. Anxiously she asked how he was, and said she was constantly praying for his safety. He put the letter in his breast pocket, summoned the Sergeant-Major and together they set off on an inspection of the trenches.

Halfway through their tour, German artillery opened fire. The two men were hurrying back towards company headquarters when Major Lucas saw a violet growing beneath a stunted tree. Thinking of his wife, he bent down to pick it up and put it in her letter. As he straightened up, the Sergeant-Major took two or three reflexive steps then crumpled in a bloody heap. His head had been blown off by a low trajectory shell from the flank.

A violet had just saved Major Lucas's life.

Or was it a Violet?

A pity she couldn't have saved the Sergeant-Major as well…

Our guardian angels, whoever or whatever they are, not only rally round at times of crisis and danger, such as war—they seem to be happy to help us in the smallest ways too. Here are two examples, taken from the almost endless supply available:

Petey, who was running The Whole Bookshop in Piccadilly, spent several weeks trying to locate a rare volume by Nikolai Roerich, the Russian traveller and mystic. As a last resort he visited a Surrey bookshop, thinking, "If it's not here, I doubt if I'll find it anywhere."

He searched the shop high and low, without success. Then, just as he was about to give up, a book fell from a top shelf and hit him on the head.

No guesses…

This final instance, more trivial perhaps, is one I treasure nonetheless:

Arriving at Pete and Bran's country cottage one afternoon,

I found them all in the garden. I admired the purple nail varnish their daughter Mandy was wearing. She ran into the house and emerged with a small bottle of the stuff, and proceeded to paint one of my nails with it, much to everyone's amusement.

I soon forgot all about it, and returned to London next morning, as I had a meeting to attend. Walking down York Street on my way to the meeting, I noticed my purple nail and swore under my breath.

At that moment my gaze fell on the window of an antique shop. Inside, at her desk, was the owner—*and sitting opposite her was a manicurist, removing the good lady's nail varnish with cotton-wool and acetone.*

As I walked on down York Street thirty seconds later, my nail restored to its original state—the manicurist had been highly amused, and refused payment for her small rescue service—I looked skyward with a grin and said out loud:

"On a scale of nought to ten, fellers, you get eleven for that one!"

Supposing that we all benefit ten times in our lives from the help of these unseen friends [ten times a week would probably be nearer the mark, but let's be really conservative] then some fifty *billion* intercessions occur in every generation!

The sheer administration required to achieve all this is enough to take one's breath away.

"The most grossly neglected energy
source on Earth is human energy. You all
possess greater powers than you imagine.
Thought, for instance: your thoughts can
heal or cripple, nourish or destroy. Wield
them wisely, always remembering that
the twin of power is responsibility."

"M"

8 HIDDEN POWERS

"Ordinary" people, the man and woman in the street, you and I, we've never had much confidence in our ability to affect the way things go. "What can *I* do about it?" has been the universal cry down the ages. We let "them" lay down the law; we let "them" decide for us, do our thinking for us.

And this, Merlin insists, is fatal.

He has repeatedly warned us not to join cults or movements of any kind; not to shout the slogans and rallying-cries of any pressure group, "lest you become a mere pawn in other people's hands. There are two dangers facing you if you don't think for yourselves," he stresses.

"On the one hand, unscrupulous people can manipulate, exploit and programme you; on the other, you surrender your individuality—the greatest gift you possess—and become sheep, swept helplessly along in the flock.

"And all the while, within every single one of you, lies a formidable array of hidden powers, which largely lie unused..."

So why don't we take a look at one or two of them?

Thought itself is a tremendously potent weapon. It is the motive power that has driven us throughout history, projecting us from primitive savagery to... well, cynics might say to the sophisticated savagery of today's nerve gases, weapon systems, and our desecration of every form of life—including our own.

It has long been known that *sound*, too, is an equally powerful tool—for good or ill. H-A once revealed to my Atlantean friends in Worcestershire that music could be used—indeed, *has* been used—to sustain or destroy entire civilisations. The persistent use of certain rhythms, intervals and harmonies, H-A confirmed, can directly affect human behaviour and emotions.

This was a major revelation to me. It set me thinking, good and hard.

Yes, of course! Why had I never thought of it before?!

National anthems, battle hymns, religious music, political

anthems, love songs, school songs, regimental marches, mantras, symphonies, Mahler, Bruckner, Elgar, Tchaikovsky, opera—the list is almost endless.

Remember Hitler's obsession with Wagner?

Stalin's fear of the music of Shostakhovich, who was branded 'undemocratic' by an iron regime that feared what it heard?

In 1967 my instructor said to me, "Do you remember how Picasso and the Cubists shattered the classical mould that had dominated art for so long? By doing so, they freed themselves and other artists—and through them, the rest of us—to look at life and reality through entirely new eyes.

"Well, at exactly the same time, black people in the Americas, oppressed and exploited by other races, discovered a subtle yet devastating weapon: their music. Consciously or unconsciously they used jazz, swing, boogie-woogie and other variations to break down—racists would say to subvert—the martial rhythms and classical structure of much of western music.

"This attracted huge numbers of sympathisers and copyists in other races, and melted down many of the barriers and hostilities between them. Operation Trojan Horse, modern style—launched this time for ultimately positive, human, spiritual purposes rather than for war…"

This was yet another startling revelation—to me, at least. [I told you it sometimes takes ages for the penny to drop.]

During my travels, I have more than once come upon the phrase "the power of the human *voice*".

Well, what *about* the human voice?

Look at World War II from this perspective, and what do we find? That one man's voice [the Führer's] galvanised an entire nation into action, with catastrophic results. Another man's voice [Churchill's] mobilised Britain, reassured oppressed Europe and helped to secure the vital support of the United States—thereby denying Hitler the realisation of his dream of a 1000-year Reich.

And reading between the lines of some of my conversations with Merlin, there is no doubt at all in my mind about who was behind that second voice...

Love?

Who would deny that, at its best, love can heal, sustain, reconcile, empower, attract, disarm, defuse and unify; or that, at it worst—and most possessive—it can stifle, cripple and destroy. Either way, it is an energy with the most phenomenally wide range of properties. One day soon, I expect they'll be able to prove it to us, scientifically.

And then there is that other, unconditional kind of love, which is a blend of wisdom, compassion, tolerance and selflessness—the kind that can lift us out of our primal state and leave us within hailing distance of the angels.

To think that all this time we've been treating "Love one another" as some kind of ridiculous spiritual platitude—a naive, idealistic and utterly impractical motto that has no meaning amid the harsh "realities" of life!

What the man who first said it knew, was this:

Love *is* the greatest power of them all; and contains within it the solution of just about every problem and crisis we have ever created—and of every mystery that still confounds us.

Then there is that other range of subtle powers we all possess, but have been conditioned by "rational" folk to ignore: our ability to contact others by thought, to heal without touching, to sense what is yet to happen, to hear inner voices, to see with our inner vision, to receive inspiration, to follow our intuition, to use our instinct, to "read" people and things.

All these gifts—for such they are—have always been used by initiates and magicians; yet they are part of the whole human being, as natural as our gifts of sight and taste and hearing.

And what is more, a little research reveals that the ancients used and relied on these powers quite naturally and without a second thought. In more recent times, only the so-called "primitive" races—Australian aboriginals, American Indians and the natives of Polynesia and Melanesia, for instance—are still using them.

It is high time we swallowed our pride, and asked these

people to share their wisdom with us—for without it, we have screwed up our relationship with the planet on the grandest scale imaginable.

Sleep, too, is the most extraordinary territory and is still largely uncharted. Captain Kirk was way off base when he called Space "the final frontier". What about sleep? The hindbrain? Our subconscious? Our unconscious? The astral planes? And the spirit worlds?!

But to return to sleep:

Throughout the sixties and seventies I found myself having innumerable precognitive dreams on the widest range of subjects, from world affairs to minor domestic matters. They were so frequent that I began to jot them down in a dream book.

Here are a few brief examples:

The divine Julie was talking to me with unusual seriousness. [If you knew her, you'd know why I call her that.] Normally she is bubbling with laughter and fun and outrageous humour, but on this occasion her gravity made a strong impression on me.

"If I get through," she said, "we've decided to postpone having a baby for a year. But if I don't get through, we'll have a baby this year if we can."

Next morning I phoned Julie and reported the dream. She could hardly believe it. She and her husband had just had a long talk about having a child, and they had agreed that if Julie passed her audition to the Royal Shakespeare Company—she did, only a few weeks later—they would postpone trying for a child...

I heard that my sister-in-law was in bed, following some sort of complications with her pregnancy. That night I had a dream that I was inside her fallopian tubes and saw a small egg falling out of position and landing with a bump in the wrong place. But the egg gave me a cheeky grin, and I instantly knew he was alright. [The face was masculine.]

In due course my sister-in-law had a healthy son, who was none the worse for the misadventure inside his mother's body. And has a notably cheeky grin.

My sister Audrey and I were on the lawn in our parents' London garden.

"She is very ill," said Audrey. "They're doing tests on her colon." She didn't say who "she" was.

Next Sunday, rather apprehensive, I visited my parents for lunch. My mother greeted me at the door.

"Bad news, I'm afraid, dear. They think Aunty Netta has cancer. They've just done some tests on her, and we're waiting to hear the results..."

My father was examining a diamond bracelet through an eyeglass. There were twin safety clasps on it, instead of the usual single one.

When I next saw my father—who had been a jeweller for more than sixty-five years—I asked him, "Have you got a bracelet with two safety clasps instead of one?"

He gave me an old-fashioned look. "As a matter of fact, I have. It came back from the workshop this week..."

Yet another example, not a dream this time [whoever arranges these things doesn't seem to mind whether we are asleep or awake]:

Strolling along the Portobello Road street market one Saturday afternoon, I wandered into a general store and bought a spatula—one of those things you use to scrape pudding or cake mixture out of the bowl—for my mother. I gave it to her the next morning, apologising for bringing her something so mundane.

She laughed, and indicated the cutlery drawer.

"Look in there. I broke my spatula last week...!"

In 1974 I wrote a screenplay of my novel *Catch The Lightning* and submitted it to Ava Gardner, whom I didn't know—but who lived in London and, I thought, would do a terrific job with the leading role.

A week or so went by, then one night I was woken by the telephone. "Hi, Michael, I love the script."

Gulp. *That* voice—at *this* hour... I checked my watch: 2.30 a.m.

"Oh, hi, Miss Gardner."

"Fuck Miss Gardner, the name's Ava."

"Er, yeah. Well that's great."

"It's a terrific idea, honey, but maybe a bit too wordy— you know, talkie-talkie—you gotta tell it in pictures."

"Absolutely. It's only a first draft. We've got lots of time to cut out all the crap."

"You got it. Well how about we meet and talk about it? Friday, six o'clock?"

"You bet. I'll be there..."

I lay awake for at least an hour, then finally fell asleep again. And had a dream. In it, I arrived at Ava's apartment near Hyde Park. She opened the door herself, we embraced, then she led me down a carpeted corridor, pushed open double doors. A dog was asleep on the huge four-poster bed.

"Out," commanded Ava. The dog gave me a dirty look and slunk out. "And this is where we'll sleep tonight," announced Ava.

I woke, my heart pounding...

Come Friday, I made my way to Knightsbridge, arrived at Ava's apartment. She opened the door herself, we embraced, then she led me down a carpeted corridor, pushed open double doors. A dog was asleep on the huge four-poster bed.

"Out," commanded Ava.

The dog, a Corgi, gave me a dirty look and slunk out.

"And this is where we'll sleep tonight," said Ava.

[No, we didn't.]

I suppose you're thinking, "That's all very well, but can you tell me who's going to win the 3.30 at Newmarket on Saturday?"

Wish I could!

Finally, here is a perfect example of those "special powers" in action, which Ava herself told me during our next telephone conversation:

I told her she had always reminded me of a witch.

She laughed. "I hope you mean a 'white' witch—*la bruja blanca?*"

"Of course," I blurted, wondering if I'd gone too far.

"Let me tell you something, honey," she went on. "A few years ago I was asleep in my hotel in Acapulco when something woke me up. I could smell gas. I got up, grabbed the dog and hurried out into the corridor. I knocked on a few doors, telling everyone to get up, there's a gas escape."

"Along comes a maid who says, 'There's no gas escape, please go back to bed, everything's fine, believe me.'"

"So reluctantly I went back to my room, and eventually fell asleep again. A few hours later I was woken by an early morning call from Madrid. One of my dearest friends had tried to kill himself in the night. He used gas..."

Ava's natural beauty and exquisite voice were second to none; she moved like a thoroughbred. Small wonder the barefoot girl from Grabtown, North Carolina grew up to play— among other, earthier roles—Venus, goddess of love, Queen Guinevere, a Russian baroness and the lonely, mysterious Empress Elizabeth of Austria. Or that one of her best directors, George Cukor, called her "the eternal woman".

And yet Ava didn't even think she could act: she would say, "Everything I ever did was a fumble."

"You're crazy," I protested. "At least a dozen of your movies prove you wrong." But she just shook her head and dismissed them all.

In her heyday, the media fed off her beauty and were hypnotised by her tempestuous private life. Here was a woman most men wanted—and many women, privately, would have loved to *be.*

One day, if there's any justice, she will be seen not just as one of the most glamorous *stars* Hollywood ever produced, but as one of the finest actresses ever to face those merciless, unblinking cameras. Her credibility was total: all the costumes, make-up and jewellery the dream factory could lay its hands on couldn't mask Ava's spirit and fire, her wit and courage.

As a woman who lived life *her* way, and rewrote the rules as she went along, she was years ahead of her time.

Her legend is intact.

She once said to me, "Honey, we may never make a picture together, but we don't have to—we work another way altogether."

We never did make *Catch The Lightning*—much to my regret, because I thought there were facets of Ava that none of her films gave her the chance to reveal—but we certainly seemed to be linked in some indefinable way.

And that applies even more so, now she has gone: the advice she continues to give me—and the outspoken, no-bull-shit way in which she gives it—is a constant source of encouragement and inspiration.

That's why, that's why the lady is a champ...

9 A CRY FROM THE HEART

One night I switched off the late evening news, halfway through the programme. I was thoroughly depressed. Nothing but bad news—wars, rumours of wars, oppression, famine, murder, rape, cruelty, breakdown of systems.

Never any good news.

Why do the media persist in thinking that good news is no news at all? We are starved of good news; we are positively longing for it. Remember VE Day? The streets of London during the Queen's Jubilee? The opening of the Los Angeles Olympic Games? The Live Aid concert? There is nothing quite like that extraordinary electricity when people gather together in the open air to celebrate, their troubles and their differences momentarily forgotten. And yet what do we see and hear on the news, every single day?

Tragedy. Suffering. Conflict and decline.

I decided to sit down and write a letter to Merlin, to get it off my chest. Silly, really, because he knows what we're thinking already—but I decided to write to him anyway. Like a child writing to Santa Claus, I wondered what address to put on the envelope. Here is my cry from the heart, dated February 1980:

"Dear Merlin,

"Everywhere we look around us today there is suffering on a titanic scale. And what makes it even more painful is that so many people have no idea that their suffering is the outcome of their own past actions, either in this lifetime or a previous one.

"Result? They are not only learning nothing from these self-inflicted wounds [being unaware of the law of Karma] but they are actually declining—becoming more and more resentful, or violent, or selfish, or apathetic, or desperate.

46

"So much so that many folk end up thinking that there can't be a God at all—or if there is, he/she can have no sense of justice or even decency, to hand out rewards and punishments so arbitrarily.

"What has brought this tragedy about? Is it the fact that vital information that is our birthright has been suppressed?

"Two of the great universal Laws have certainly been hidden from us by successive regimes. This has been going on for so long that today's authorities are probably quite unaware of them.

"Forgive me for trying to define these two Laws to you of all people, Merlin—you probably had something to do with drafting them in the first place! It's just my way of thinking aloud:

"The first is the law of Karma, the law of cause and effect, call it what we will. It states that every action has a reaction—and so, everything we do returns to us. No-one *imposes* this law on us: it is a totally natural phenomenon.

"The second is the law of Reincarnation. Again, not a piece of legislation so much as a fact of life. As I understand it, the purpose of our existence is to gain experience of life on all levels, to gain wisdom and eventually to return to our Source, adding the sum of our adventures to it.

"To make this possible, we commute between higher worlds and the physical Universe. No-one can learn all that physical life has to teach in one lifetime, so we revisit Earth many times and enjoy the comparative freedom of the higher planes between each incarnation.

"And until every human being on Earth is told of these two laws, the tragedy will continue. The moment we know of cause and effect and rebirth, many other mysteries and apparent injustices are explained. We can begin to clean up our act at every level, from the personal to the planetary.

"So now to my special request:

"As things stand, many millions of people are suffering, and will continue to suffer—often without having the slightest idea why—*for the rest of their lives*. Why cannot the pain, the physical hardships and disabilities, or the endless run of appalling 'luck' or 'accidents' or failure or frustration begin to ease up *during their lifetime*?

"There are several reasons why this reprieve, if more common than it is now, would have great value:

"First, it would teach those who struggle to improve their lives and themselves that effort and self-discipline and persistence *can* pay off old debts and earn a remission of sentence, as it were.

"Secondly, it would teach those who saw our suffering, our efforts and our eventual reward: they might even be encouraged to try to re-shape their *own* lives.

"Thirdly, much of the growing anger, bitterness, violence and ever-*increasing* bad karma would be evaporated. What can it possibly serve if millions of human beings who have a painful lesson to learn, or an old debt to pay off, incarnate with some disability or disadvantage, don't consciously know *why*, live lives of pain, growing resentment and hopelessness, and end their lives *worse off than ever*?!

"It's much the same as slinging offenders into prisons which are nothing more than incubators of crime, violence and revenge: they emerge, in many cases, far worse off than when they entered...

"And finally, a great deal of administration on the inner planes would be avoided, or at least simplified, if we were able to pay off certain bad debts in our present lifetime—and so return home with our slates clean, or at least cleaner.

"Millions of people at present are returning to the higher worlds in a *worse* spiritual condition than when they were born here. Surely this cannot be part of the Plan?!

"Yours very respectfully,

Michael."

I sealed this rather impetuous and probably misguided, but nonetheless heartfelt letter in an envelope, and propped it in a corner of my room among some pieces of quartz, citrine and a Siberian amethyst which I treasure for their practical purposes as well as their ornamental value. A day or so later, after supper, I tuned in, pen poised, and waited for an answer.

At last the pen began to write, slowly at first, then with gathering speed:

"Most of you are indeed finding your present life a tough one. Many karmic debts are being settled: the Grand Audit is under weigh, so that the books may be balanced before the next Act in the cosmic drama begins.

"If you could somehow detach yourself and survey

your own progress along the path during this and previous lifetimes, you would discover that individual successes and failures, triumphs and tragedies are far less significant than they appear in close-up— that is, when you are actually experiencing them.

"The only thing that ultimately matters is your overall progress, your ability to learn from the rewards and obstacles you place in your path. Never forget, in almost every instance it is *your own soul* that places them there, no-one else.

"No success that we have is supreme, and no failure irreparable. All is part and parcel of our onward journey through many lives and conditions. We prefer ease and success, but our higher self, knowing better, often confronts us with tests and obstacles—to see how we handle them.

"Sometimes you feel that life is collapsing around you. You wonder how much *more* pain and disappointment you and others will have to endure. Try, if you can—it isn't easy, I know—to detach yourself from the whole episode; watch yourself going through it as if it were a play; then shrug, smile and move on.

"A crisis can provide a perfect opportunity to pay off old karmic debts; it can also be our soul's way of trying to tell us that it is time for a change in direction, or time to put our mettle to the test, or that we've learnt all we can in one particular field and it's time to enter another.

"Success teaches us little in the long run. On the contrary, it can be dangerous by breeding vanity and complacency and tempting false friends to bask in our reflected glory. In the past, how many despots and rulers have employed courtiers to flatter them; how many of today's so-called 'superstars' still do… "Remember when that young American friend of yours said, 'What a pity life always serves it up in two flavors'? Well, with respect, he was wrong—because we are only really tested when the going gets tough.

"Yes, the Laws of karma and rebirth must be taught to every child—and every adult, too. Yes, those who have suppressed these and other truths have much to answer for—and will surely answer for it. Yet even this tragedy has played its part in the overall scheme of things.

"For the moment, I shall ask you to take this on trust. It is not the first time I have done so, nor will it be the last. In time you will know why I do so.

"As for the rest, the only thing that will end the darkness on Earth is light. And the light is in *you*. So switch it on. One by one, all of you. Even the leaders of the nations. *Especially* the leaders. And presto! The darkness will have vanished. Forever."

"We have all known pain, and somehow survived it. We have all caused pain, and come to regret it. By absorbing some of the pain of this world and that of our fellow man—and by giving it back, not as anger, violence and a desire for revenge, but as wisdom and love and experience—we become alchemists, true magicians; no longer part of the problem, but of the solution."

"M"

3. THE GUARDIANS

10 FRIENDS IN HIGH PLACES

From the moment Merlin materialised in Pete's Hertfordshire bedroom on that first memorable night, Pete began to develop at a remarkable rate. The agnostic cameraman swiftly became an accomplished dowser and geomancer. It was as if the Magician's closeness had lifted several veils, revealing to Pete what he already knew deep within him: the work he had done in one particular previous incarnation—and what he is capable of in this one.

He began to travel round England, attuning to ancient power sites and aligning energies. Sometimes he took crystals with him, at others a stave banded in copper, silver and gold.

Whenever I accompanied him on these expeditions, I let him decide what to do, and served as an assistant, or supplementary power pack. The night sky was a rich source of illumination, in every sense of the word. With "M"'s guidance, we learned of three prime energies that permeate all our lives, and the specific constellations related to them:

The Magician: emblem, the Wand; constellation, Ursa Major [the Plough]; keynote, creative intelligence.

The Lady: emblem, the Cup or chalice; constellation, Cassiopeia; keynote, love/wisdom.

The King: emblem, the Sword; constellation, Draco [the Dragon]; keynote, will.

We began to familiarise ourselves with each of these energies, and found ourselves referring to them as "the Guardians". Pete demonstrated an astonishing ability to communicate with their star groups. He would stand in the meadow behind his cottage, lift the stave towards one of the constellations—and almost immediately a shooting star would leave it and flash across the night sky.

One night, I was horsing around and not concentrating.

54

"There! D'you see it?" Pete cried, three times in succession. On each occasion my attention had been elsewhere.

Pete marched up to me, stood me facing east, tilted my head towards Cassiopeia. "Don't move!" he commanded.

I stood stock still as he aimed the stave.

A moment later, a brilliant shooting star left Cassiopeia, streaked across the northern sky, passed the Plough and disappeared in the heart of Draco.

"Well?" challenged Pete.

"Jeeeeezuss!" I exclaimed, gaping like a six-year-old.

Pete was not only on excellent terms with the constellations: almost overnight he had developed an extraordinary rapport with Nature, especially with trees.

One Spring Equinox, he and I visited Ringshall, near Ivinghoe Beacon. In the heart of the wood we had discovered two mighty beech trees, hundreds of years old, which we had dubbed "the Lord and Lady of the forest". The wedding of Prince Charles was coming up, and hilltop bonfires were being lit throughout Britain.

For some while we had been wondering about the security surrounding the Prince, and decided we should consult the two venerable beeches. They came up with something very dramatic: explosives would soon be discovered in or near Buckingham Palace. "But don't alert the authorities," the trees added. "It isn't as serious as it sounds."

Sure enough, a few days later gelignite was found in a van belonging to a member of the Buckingham Palace ground staff. But it was innocent enough: the man confessed he used it for poaching trout and salmon.

As if to balance this unsavoury news, the trees gave Pete a second message:

"Many of your telephone messages travel along wires slung from telegraph poles, don't they? And telegraph poles were once trees, weren't they? Well if you have an important message to send to someone far afield, why not ask *us*—and we will send the message from tree to tree across country, at great speed—and no cost!"

"And why not?" we thought. All it would take was some-one receptive enough to pick up the message at the other end!

"The constellations of the Zodiac could be regarded as twelve seats at the Round Table. You will have ample opportunity to master the attributes of each sign, and so emerge, in time, as a whole being, embodying all their complementary qualities. These twelve labours are an initiation that all human beings must undergo."

"M"

11 ENTER THE KING

In 1973, Petey gave me a copy of Alice Bailey's *Initiation, Human and Solar*, and almost at once the book fell open at a diagram of the three prime rays or energies relayed to Earth by the Sun, a giant transformer which receives these energies from "further up the line" and steps them down so that we can assimilate them:

Ray 1: Will

Ray 2: Love/wisdom

Ray 3: Creative intelligence

Petey said I was a Ray 1 character, and I saw no reason to disagree: I have always identified with the idea of will and purpose and order. It has taken me years to develop the other two, and so create a balance of sorts.

Back in 1961, a particularly testing time of my life, I had become aware of what I can only describe as a kinglike or Christlike being. He would just "be there" when things got really tough and I came close to giving up. And once, when I desperately called him to help a friend of mine who was running off the rails, he actually materialised behind me as I glanced into a mirror—but only for a moment.

And maybe this, too, is evidence of the influence of the "King" energy re-entering my life:

Between 1967 and 1971, while my instructor and I were having our usual Sunday evening conversations, he would occasionally look behind me and tell me I had a "visitor".

These visitors were always military men. During this period I was visited by Field Marshal Earl Alexander of Tunis—whom I had briefly met while doing manoeuvres on Salisbury Plain, several years before; Field Marshal Slim, Lord Gort, Lord Auchinleck, Lord Wavell and several others.

Mystified, I asked why they were dropping in like this. The answer was always the same:

"You are a soldier. You have a soldier's work to do. They are here to give you strength and discipline; to teach you the importance of strategy and planning, which you are going to need in days to come."

Which mystified me even more—because ever since my National Service days I had always considered myself the most unlikely soldier imaginable, since the profession of war is something I have always found totally alien.

In this lifetime, at least...

"Consider how Will, Love/wisdom and Intelligence unify and sustain all things, from the dance of the smallest electron to the majestic procession of the galaxies. How could it be otherwise?"

"M"

12 ENTER THE LADY

In the late summer of 1967—that unforgettable year, crowned by the *Sergeant Pepper* album—I was sitting with my instructor——

Forgive me for breaking off in mid-sentence, but one of those mind-blowing coincidences, so-called, has just occurred:

At the very moment I was word-processing the above words, the television newsreader announced that my instructor and his sister have been found dead, of natural causes, in their east London apartment.

A man of extraordinary powers, my teacher has even managed to let me know of his passing—of which I might otherwise have remained unaware, as we often didn't meet for months on end.

But to return to the story:

I was sitting with my instructor and his sister, when he suddenly stopped speaking and gazed into the corner of the room behind me. After a few moments he announced that "the Holy Lady" was approaching with a number of attendants.

I asked who she was.

"The feminine aspect of God," he replied. "The instrument of the supreme Nature power; the intelligence of Nature that has been worshipped under different names throughout history."

I wondered why she was visiting us.

"She says she has reviewed your lives on the akashic record," he went on, answering my unspoken question. "She tells me you have unconsciously worshipped her throughout your lives, and you have spent much of your present life looking for an ideal woman."

I suddenly remembered that ever since I was a small boy, I have been trying to draw or paint a woman's face—an idealised face, perfect yet real—but it always eludes me.

"She is saying that she is aware of what you are trying to achieve, and has now become your patron. But she will not

61

allow your work to come to fruition until it is as near perfect as can be. Should you ever need someone to help you revise or complete any project, she will see that they come to you. She gives you her blessing, and says she will leave a sign of her visit. She is leaving now."

Rather shyly, I thanked her for her visit and for her help.

When she had gone, my instructor said that this was only the third time he had encountered the Lady. "Well, chum, you've got some friends in *very* high places. Don't let it go to your head."

That night I went home, undressed and got into bed.

A star was shining down on me out of the darkness.

I turned on the light and examined the ceiling closely. A year before, I had stuck a number of luminous stars to the ceiling, but six months later my apartment had been redecorated and the stars had all vanished beneath two layers of paint.

But the paint had now been removed from the largest of these stars!

I got back into bed and stared at it for several minutes, remembering the Lady's visit, and her promise.

From out of the blue, with no warning whatsoever, a second major influence had come into my life. Until the Lady put in her appearance, I was half a person, unaware of the real importance of feminine energy and natural wisdom. But ever since that evening, I have tended to see history and the mounting catalogue of world crises from the woman's perspective rather than from the man's.

As every day passes I grow more and more convinced that the "fall of Man" dates from the time when men stopped listening to women—if they ever did. The Adam and Eve story casts Eve as the heavy, but I reckon that's a disgraceful slander, rigged by the elders of the Church to keep women in their place. The same was to happen to Mary Magdalene and Morgan le Fay, but that is another story.

The imbalance caused by male supremacy is particularly acute now—when the feminine viewpoint is given almost no weight in the world.

And as Merlin himself once said to Pete and me, "Is it not high time that the Earth herself were represented in your council chambers?

"Seek the Light,

See the Light,

Feel the Light,

Be the Light."

I believe that the above message, whispered to me as I sat enchanted by the snowdrops growing in the woods behind Hartland Abbey in north Devon, was from the Lady. It seems to sum up the whole purpose of human existence, in only twelve words. A neat feat of compression, I think you'll agree!

13 ENTER THE MASTER OF CEREMONIES

In the fall of 1981 Pete telephoned me and asked me to visit him. He sounded rather excited. I always enjoyed my expeditions to his cottage in Hertfordshire, so I set off at once.

Pete had done a lot of research into the three prime Guardian energies; but now, prompted by Merlin to dig a bit deeper and study the night sky, he had discovered a *fourth* energy. Like the other three it had been under our noses all the time, maybe too close for us to see or identify it.

This fourth energy seems to emanate from the constellation of Orion. He is the Lord of dance, theatre, circus, ritual, art, humour and spontaneity. The Joker in the pack. His function is directly opposite to that of the King, who represents order. Two well-remembered ancient Roman festivals carry all the hallmarks of this energy: the Bacchanalia, drunken revels in honour of Bacchus, god of wine; and the Saturnalia, the festival of Saturn celebrated by all classes.

Presumably the powers-that-be allowed these revelries as they provided a useful safety-valve for the release of pent-up emotions and appetites. Just once a year, masters would serve their servants; the lowliest could become king or queen for a day. But by organising these festivities on a strict once-a-year basis, the State undermined this impulse, diluted it, turned it into something ritualistic.

History tells us that the powers-that-be are none too fond of riotous assemblies, even happy ones, and so this freewheeling energy has been persistently frowned on and discouraged—except on specified national holidays.

And yet this impulse for self-expression is a vital one, a perfect complement to the discipline and order of the King. Did not kings have their jesters throughout the Middle Ages?!

We *need* our laughter, our music and dance, our festivals. We need an occasional release from the pressures of everyday life; we need to get away from it all, to hang loose, to kick over the traces and fool about.

My Australian sister-in-law, Christine, recently said to me,

"We all have an external, practical self who looks after everything, makes rules, creates routines and obeys them. But there is this other, inner self who is something else altogether. It has *no* rules or routines, it is *not* the slave of convention or time or propriety. It demands attention, needs to be nourished, and we ignore it at our peril."

I heartily agreed. Christine continued: "A child is almost entirely this inner self—it is a free spirit, impulsive, open, imaginative, unorganised, sometimes destructive, unpredictable—and then comes the process of imposing on it an outer, responsible, disciplined, socially acceptable self. And in all too many cases, the free spirit inside the child is inhibited, repressed, smothered and, finally, killed."

The Master of Ceremonies has an all-important creative function too. He is the impulse behind everyone who invents, writes, experiments, dances and makes music. The Muses who inspire us are his agents. He is the spirit of laughter and comedy and companionship, the unacknowledged patron of loners, pioneers, originals and eccentrics.

Looking back, I have to admit that I have served my inner self ever since I can remember—often to the detriment of that outer me who was expected to build a career, earn money, achieve status and do all the other conventional things. I can really sympathise with my parents' distress and disappointment. And yet, years ago, *without knowing why*, I turned down several very attractive openings and decided instead to plough my own furrow, wherever it led.

It has turned out to be a long and winding road with many hazards and insecurities. But at last the pieces of the jigsaw puzzle are beginning to come together, and ultimately I have no regrets. I have learned more, I suspect, than if I had taken one of the more comfortable options once open to me.

On the other hand, I know several people who have suppressed their inner selves—and paid dearly for it. It is as if they fear it, mistrust it, feel their "real" world threatened by its sudden, powerful urges.

Yet this is no hidden dragon or monster trying to break out of its cage and wreak havoc. It is our spirit that *knows* it is

66

free, and knows that its warder, our outer self, is the prisoner.

Only recently did I realise, for what it's worth, that all four Guardian energies arrived in my life at exact seven-year intervals: in 1960, the King; in 1967, the Lady; in 1974, Merlin; and in 1981, the Master of Ceremonies.

Pete, however, has other ideas. He once told me, "When you were a small and lonely child in short trousers, bib and braces, you met the Lady in a country lane. She held your hand and spoke to you of many things, most of which you didn't really understand. And you chattered away to her, nineteen to the dozen. Some things never change!

"A few years later the King made his presence felt, but not in person this time—he used an older man, a teacher or uncle, perhaps, who said something that made a profound impression on you.

"As for Merlin himself, he tells me that over a period of years he entered your dreams and showed you things you only half-remembered when you woke up. He was preparing you for a time when you would be working with him again. And that time, I need hardly tell you, is now!"

To be honest, I have no memory at all of meeting the Lady as a child. But as for the King using an older man to communicate something to me, there *is* one person who fits the bill perfectly: my late headmaster, who said something at the end of my final report that took me over twenty years to decipher; something that told me that one person, at least, had seen right inside me and wasn't fooled by the volatile persona I had already created for myself in self-defence; something that even hinted at the quest I was to embark on, much later.

How did he *know*?!

And as for Merlin, finding him in Park Wood was one of the most natural things I have ever done, so I can well believe that he had prepared me for our reunion long in advance. No wonder I had such extraordinary dreams in the 1960s and 1970s!

I am profoundly grateful to all four Guardians for just being there. It makes all the struggles and heart-aches worthwhile, knowing we have such powerful allies to call on when the going gets rough. Whether they are part of our higher selves or ascended beings or universal energies seems to me to be immaterial. One thing is certain: their help and guidance is boundless, and they themselves—if we can only clear a channel for them in our receivers—are everpresent.

It is tempting for most males to identify solely with the King, and to regard love/wisdom and even creative intelligence as irrelevant. Indeed, the dangerous imbalance in our society has come about precisely because men regard the gentler qualities—compassion, consideration, caring—as effeminate.

And yet the *whole* man—ask virtually any woman—is someone whose masculinity is finely balanced with gentler qualities.

Becoming aware of the Guardians doesn't make us special in any way—they are universal, and available to anyone—nor does contact with them give us immunity from natural laws: if we stick our fingers in the fire, we still get burned; if we keep on making the same mistakes, the penalties still increase. In fact, having encountered the Guardians, we have less excuse for screwing things up than most other people.

No wonder Merlin always says, "Remember, the twin of privilege is responsibility."

In ancient times—in Atlantis, for example, and at the height of the Egyptian civilisation—rulers are said to have been the representatives on Earth of these divine archetypes.

Kings, pharaohs and other rulers would embody all the finer attributes of masculine power, will and justice. Queens and empresses would personify the high feminine principles of love, wisdom and mercy.

As time passed, these ideals were largely forgotten and, as history shows us, countless subsequent rulers, who simply succeeded their fathers or attained power by force or cunning, have been little more than despots or decadents, obsessed by power and riddled with greed, ambition or vice.

It can be no accident that the monarchy in Britain has attained an unparalleled degree of popularity during the lifetime of the present Queen and her parents, who attained the throne by chance and, despite their initial reluctance, went on to embody all the qualities of duty, example and service that the monarchy is intended to enshrine. That this should have occurred at a time of social ferment and decline is something of a paradox.

There are those who wonder if the British monarchy has any relevance in this century. Yet if it were abolished, the role of standard-bearer of the nation's ideals would devolve on each successive President or Prime Minister—whose climb to power would almost inevitably oblige him, or her, to sacrifice the human decencies which the Queen, with little or no temporal power, has personified throughout her reign.

In view of Anglo-American history, it is richly ironic that a solitary American woman should have been directly responsible for averting a major constitutional crisis [there is mounting evidence that the one she caused was far less damaging than the one that would almost certainly have arisen had she *not* arrived on the scene] thereby enabling the Crown to attain its present position.

14 ANOTHER PROMISE FULFILLED

Some years ago I wrote three related screenplays about this crucial phase in human history. You'll think I'm crazy, but I reckoned that we might be able to avert Armageddon if we acted it out in all its horror on the big screen!

The second movie in the sequence, *Battle for the Earth*, dramatises the final conflict between the dark side of our nature and the other one. Set in the near future, it reaches its climax when war breaks out between nations employing a range of satellite-launched missiles. A number of cities are destroyed. Holes are torn in the ionosphere by ray weapons, exposing the planet to lethal concentrations of cosmic rays.

The writing is now well and truly on the wall.

The leader of a civilian Special Forces group with connections in the White House contacts the President and advises him that only one thing might avert total disaster:

> BEN
> [into the phone]
> I reckon we've got one last card to play, sir. Can you set up the biggest prayer drive the planet's ever seen? Every damn country you can reach— China and the Soviet Union included. It doesn't matter what they do or don't believe. If a billion people can spend the next few hours sending out the powerfullest thoughts they've ever had, there *might* be a chance. The Russians'll understand: it's nuclear energy we've got to have—a man-made chain reaction!
>
> THE PRESIDENT
> [into phone]
> Consider it done.

A montage follows, showing huge crowds gathering in silence throughout the world, to invoke help. Help arrives. In the shape of the GUARDIAN:

High above the Earth hangs a vast multicoloured globe of LIGHT, with a corona of dazzling brilliance. Radiating from it are rays or filaments of light, gossamer-fine.

The VISITOR gives off an aura of infinite power and benevolence—a pure male energy and will offset by ineluctable feminine love and wisdom, and an intelligence that embraces them both.

The GUARDIAN's work begins—portions of this scintillating star break off and speed away in several directions. First the auroral storms—deceptively beautiful wounds in the Earth's protective shield—are surrounded by the GUARDIAN's lesser selves and irradiated in a brief, dazzling conflict until they fade and disappear.

Then these smaller spheres descend on all the nuclear and other naval, military and air force installations and render the world's offensive weaponry inoperable.

Now the GUARDIAN, speaking through BEN, says he will address the world, using television networks, at 6 p.m. GMT.

So, this celestial visitor, having put an end to the mayhem, is going to speak to the world, is he?
What is he going to say?!
Oh well, better call you-know-who again. He did say call him whenever I got into trouble, remember?
So I did.
On a sunny afternoon I went to that seat in Regent's Park,

took out pen and paper, closed my eyes for a moment and sent a wire to High Command.

Merlin was as good as his word: within thirty seconds my pen was flying across the page, and eight minutes later the Guardian's speech was written. And I've never changed a word of it, from that day to this.

When my friends read the finished screenplay of *Battle*, they said, "Why not make a promotional tape of the Guardian's speech with music and effects—the way we did with *Links With Space*?"

Great idea. I asked Pete Carbines if he'd perform his usual magic and engineer the thing for us. He agreed.

Next problem: where on Earth do we find a voice powerful enough to play the Guardian? Answer: *nowhere* on Earth! I'll ask "M" if he'll do it for us.

I went haring up to Hertfordshire, to consult Pete. That night, "M" came through as usual. We talked of many things then, just before he left us, I asked if he would do me a great favour.

"Ask," he said in that deep, sonorous voice.

"Er, Merlin, I've just finished this screenplay, *Battle For The Earth*, and for the climax of the picture I've written this speech for a character called the Guardian who——"

"*Who's* just written this speech by the Guardian?!" thundered "M", who has the best line in mock outrage you'll ever hear.

I laughed. "Yeah, point taken. Sorry about that. Well anyway, we've decided to make a tape of it, with music and effects. Would you be very kind, if Pete comes to our recording studio one night soon, and do the Guardian's voice for us?"

There was a moment of silence as the Archmage considered this request. Then:

"I shall rehearse!"

Again I burst out laughing—with relief, mostly—knowing that the recording session was going to be something else altogether.

It was a dark and stormy night—what else?—when Pete

and Bran drove down from Hertfordshire in their old banger. They picked me up and we drove south. Rain lashed down; lightning—yes, *purple* lightning—heralded thunder that sounded like an artillery bombardment.

At Pete Carbines' house we dried ourselves, had a reviving cup of tea and went up to his attic bedroom-cum-studio, a tiny room stacked from floor to ceiling with recording equipment, books, tapes and other paraphernalia.

Somehow we all fitted into this confined space. Rain and wind rattled the windows—hardly the ideal conditions for a recording session, I thought. I should have known better.

Peter Quiller took his place at the microphone—one of those irreplaceable BBC mikes from the 1940s. I handed him the two pages of script, he looked cursorily at them then shut his eyes to prepare.

As if a signal had been given, the wind died, the rain stopped.

Pete Carbines nodded, indicating "Go."

And Merlin, as you have already guessed, did the entire speech, syllable perfect, in one take.

And Pete's eyes were closed throughout the recording.

Sounds of war, destruction and chaos rise to a terrifying climax, then fade to silence. Now we hear a new sound—just as awesome but in an entirely different way—announcing the arrival of the celestial visitor. At last he speaks:

THE GUARDIAN
We are the Guardian. We have been watching over you since your infancy—sometimes with pleasure, at others with dismay. When you stumbled and lost your way, we sent you helpers. Most of them you didn't even recognise. Some you accepted, but even these you buried in ritual and dogma…

You have advanced quickly in the last one hundred years—too quickly, perhaps: your heads have left your hearts behind. What is knowledge without wisdom to apply it? You dream unending dreams of conquest, domination— yet you have not even conquered *yourselves*...

You were given this green and pleasant world for a purpose, and that purpose you must fulfill. Your weapons of destruction we have frozen in time. They are now out of your reach—as far out of your reach as yesterday or tomorrow. There they will remain for seven years. If, at the end of that time, you want them back again, you shall have them...

The real battle for the Earth is not being waged in Space, but in your own minds. Think deeply on this. Never forget how great is the power of your thought...

Do not mourn your dead—there *is* no death: those who have left you live on in a neighbouring Universe. Gather your wounded together—they will receive healing before we go...

Leave the destroyed cities as monuments to the past. Build new ones. Other tests lie before you, but you will be equal to them...

It is your destiny, one day, to join us. One day, like us, you will guide younger worlds. And so it goes on, in a perfect spiral…

Respect the planet who supplies all your needs. Serve each other, and share your strengths. Set your feet on the upward path. We shall always be with you…

We wish you a fleeting glimpse of the glorious future that awaits you all. May the light of peace, joy, love and wisdom be with you all, now and for ever more.

4. OPERATION EXCALIBUR

15 THE CIRCLE OF LIGHT

One thing you will probably have noticed in your own life: this questing business is nothing like those linear journeys that go from A to B to C, like a train along predetermined tracks.

To trace your progress you have to keep going backwards and forwards in time, as they sometimes do in movies, revealing layer after layer of cause and effect. It also goes in fits and starts and, more often than not, has to take second place to other, more mundane, activities such as trying to make a living, paying bills and running our lives.

If the truth be known, all of us began our journey of discovery lifetimes ago, and will only hit the finishing tape after many more lifetimes to come.

One phenomenon my friends and I have noticed in recent years is that odd pieces of the jigsaw keep dropping into place.

You don't realise just how many until you look back a few years.

Only then, when you add them all up, do you realise how much has happened.

Three years before Merlin's dramatic reappearance, Simon came to see me, excited about a book he was reading: John Michell's *City of Revelation*. A study of Britain's secred landscape, it is a companion to his classic, *The View Over Atlantis*.

The passage Simon wanted to show me describes a huge circle that is imprinted on the west of England. Around its perimeter lie such key sites as Stonehenge and Glastonbury Tor. The center of the circle, John Michell calculated, lies in the Malvern Hills, where the three counties of Herefordshire, Gloucestershire and Worcestershire meet.

I was already hooked:

I *knew* this place!

At the outbreak of World War II my brother, sister and I had been evacuated to a lodge on an estate at the foot of the Malvern Hills. As children, we had scampered happily up the side of the first of these hills and gazed out over the immense surrounding plain.

A close friend, Tony Standcumbe, and I drove down to the lodge, where we were greeted ecstatically by Bill and Elsie Devereux, who had looked after us so well, all those years ago—and who looked exactly as I remembered them. Later that afternoon they regaled us with a high tea of scones, sandwiches and icing cakes—just like the ones we had enjoyed as children.

Next morning we drove the two miles up to White Leafed Oak, a scattering of white-painted houses nestling between the first two hills, where the three counties meet.

Tony's little Saab struggled up the last few yards and pulled up gratefully in the little hollow, opposite a long, low, lath-and-plaster cottage, once a cider mill. We lowered the windows and sat for a while in the almost supernatural silence.

Towering above us to the right was the grassy flank of Chase End Hill, southernmost of the range. In front of us rose the tree-clad slope of Ragged Stone Hill, its summit hidden from view.

It was as if we had left the present day and entered medieval England. Arthur's England. Steep roofs, once thatched, log-piles, a moss-covered orchard clinging to the hillside. As the car bounced up the last hundred yards, a herd of sows had come trotting across the rich red mud of their paddock to greet us like old friends.

Three years later, after we had returned several times to White Leafed Oak, I wrote the screenplay *Catch The Lightning*, and set my leading character right here in the cider mill cottage. And when we scoured England for a castle in which to shoot sequences of the American envoy with the Foreign Secretary, the only suitable one in all the land turned out to be Eastnor Castle, which lies only four miles from White Leafed Oak, in the shadow of the Malverns! Another piece of the jigsaw.

Describing White Leafed Oak in the novelisation of *Catch The Lightning*, I later wrote:

Time has stood still here for centuries. Kings, empires, wars and revolutions have come and gone, but life in this sleepy hollow drifts along at its own

78

sweet pace, unchanged and unchanging. It is a place where lambs graze beneath the apple trees, plaster gnomes squat on outsize toadstools and undismayed rabbits watch you go by before bouncing away into the undergrowth.

Unknown to most people it is a sacred place, lying as it does at the exact centre of a great circle around whose perimeter, at equidistant points, lie such ancient sites as Stonehenge and Glastonbury Tor.

The circle is a wheel of immense power, installed by nameless master builders long before the present race emerged, and now lying dormant.

But for the moment, there sat Tony and I, grinning broad and silly grins that wanted to explode into laughter.

We both had an overpowering feeling that we had just come home.

That fall, I asked our Atlantean friends, who were then living in Cheltenham—though now they have a lovely estate on the western slopes of the Malverns—if they'd meet us at White Leafed Oak on the day of the equinox, and help us locate the precise centre of the great Circle.

One of the Atlanteans, Jacqueline Thorburn, an experienced geomancer, told us that the summit of Ragged Stone Hill was what we were looking for. She also reminded us of a local legend:

"Whoever sleeps on Ragged Stone hill, never wakes." We decided that was probably just a device to keep unwanted people away, and set off.

A robin welcomed us as we entered the wood at the foot of the hill—a courtesy we have enjoyed every time we return to the place.

Half an hour later, breathless after trudging long, steep paths lined by gorse and foxgloves, we climbed onto the summit and stood in a circle round the guardian rock.

We closed our eyes and Jacqueline recited a simple invocation. She looked like an ancient Egyptian high priestess who had stepped out of her own own time into another.

I opened my eyes for a moment.

The light had turned silvery blue. Over each of my companions a shimmering angelic figure stood on guard.

And above us all stood the incandescent figure of a woman clothed in light—immense, at least thirty feet high.

Surely this was the Holy Lady herself!

I shut my eyes again and waited until Jacqueline brought the little ceremony to an end.

Ever since, I have associated that hilltop with the feminine ray or energy. It is unquestionably a place of great spiritual potency, both incoming and outpouring.

Petey later described this Circle of Light, as I have come to call it, as "in a sense, the Grail of Britain". The view from the summit rock at its centre is one of the most breath-taking sights in all the land.

We were not the least surprised to learn that Elgar, Vaughan Williams and Gustav Holst had all lived and worked on or near the Malverns. Their quintessentially English music no doubt derives much of its power and subtlety from the place. Walk these hills in any weather, and you will know why—if not how—*The Planets Suite* came into being.

One summer, we decided to greet the solstice moment on the top of Ragged Stone hill—even though it occurred at sunrise.

We drove from London, arrived at the foot of the Malverns in the dark, were guided for two miles by a white owl that flew in the beam of our headlights and led us to a small concealed turning that wound up to the hollow—thanks again, Merlin!—climbed the hill with the aid of torches, and waited.

The moment of sunrise that followed was so memorable that it, too, found its way into *Catch The Lightning*:

> Melinda slept until first light, and woke up thoroughly refreshed. Unhurriedly she dressed and went outside into the cool stillness of dawn, wearing a woollen cape against the chilly air.
>
> Soon she was pushing her way through the

shoulder-high ferns, past a guard of honour of tall mauve foxgloves, glad of the narrow, almost invisible path generations of visitors had beaten. Fifty feet from the summit, the fern wall abruptly ended. She clambered up the last few yards and stood for a while to recover her breath.

Then she stepped up onto the guardian rock.

Far below her the ageless plain waited, breathless and expectant in the pearly half-light. Behind her, several hundred feet below, stood the Castle in its wooded park, the flags of the nations flying from its four towers.

The spine of the hills, running away north to Worcestershire Beacon, jutted out of the plain like the ridged back of a giant sleeping dragon, sheltering several villages on either side, and the cathedral town of Malvern to the east.

At her feet, two counties stretched towards the horizon, a chequerboard of greens and ochre studded with toy villages, sharpened-pencil spires and a lattice of hedges and roads. And twenty miles to the west, a faint blue smudge of mountains that was Wales.

She closed her eyes and let the peace and stillness fill her. Then, sensing a change in the light, reopened her eyes.

A blazing red-gold spacecraft was hovering over the dark band of cloud that lined the horizon. It was the upper half of the sun. An invading sea of mist was rolling across the plain, breaking against two distant hills like waves in ultra-slow motion. Into the orchestrated silence came a piping woodwind chorus from the birds, and an occasional brassy blare of cattle and sheep.

It was a world at the dawn of Creation. Or a world awaiting a new dispensation. So perfect, so immaculate, so complete that, despite herself, she wanted to laugh and shout and dance.

Slowly, majestically, the brilliant silvergold sun rose above the band of cloud, an all-seeing, all-knowing eye.

Something made Melinda turn and look behind her. High in the sky above the Castle, two vast pink clouds hung like an Archangel's wings upraised to invoke? announce? authorise and bless? the coming day.

"With cosmic timing set when Earth was young, the pause approaches. The inevitability of growth accounted for, and the hesitancy of enquiring intelligence understood, the sweeping silence builds as all life forces prepare and tune to the greatest frequency in Creation.

"Hearken, Earth! Stand outside your incessant clamour and listen. Drop the useless possessions and reach for the tools of survival, those that are truly of value to your children. Await the coming together of forces never dreamed in your early misguided clutching for atomic understanding.

"Imagine the frequency of your planet. The very soil you rape is alive with the power that links galaxies and stabilises the empyreal grid. Manifestation is close. Stellar stairways in space await your feet when they tread the path of the lamb.

"As it was in the beginning is NOW and ever shall be. Follow the doves. Adjustments must be made."

Simon received this transmission in the spring of 1973 from someone using the call-sign "Dragonfly". I believe it could have been a message from Merlin or one of his agents, alerting us to the need for immediate change, within and around us.

16 A MIDSUMMER MOMENT

Our very next visit to that hilltop was equally memorable, but in quite another way:

To celebrate the next midsummer solstice, eight of us revisited Ragged Stone Hill. We stood in a circle around the guardian rock and Petey recited the Great Invocation. As he reached the last line—"Let Light and love and power restore the Plan on Earth"—we raised our arms in the usual way. Or rather, we *tried* to raise them. But a sudden pillar of energy, glowing gold and silver and pink and blue, was pouring down into the hill from above—and none of us could move!

We all "saw" and felt this colossal, benevolent power and happily let it flood through us. Then, as suddenly as it had arrived, it was gone. We stepped back from the summit rock, gasping and laughing.

Petey said quietly, "I think something rather important has just happened." Which for him, who is the soul of modesty and hates pretension of any kind, was really saying something.

Back in London, I decided to ask Wellesley Tudor Pole if he could tell us what had happened. He was one of the initiates who advised Churchill behind the scenes during World War II. A few days later I had his answer, channelled by Lady Cynthia Sandys and transcribed by a dear friend, Rosamond Lehmann:

> "Now for the message I am told to give you. Since the summer solstice, on the very eve of the great power-giving moment, the centre of the Earth opened, releasing many new and hitherto unknown rays and forces onto your plane.
>
> "As seen with the inner sight, it was like a huge earthquake or eruption coming without sound, but with a blinding light, and a scent of flowers unknown to you.
>
> "All this has been engineered by the great Nature

spirits in order to parry the man-made forces of pollution. Now these rays are beautiful, vital and God-given, but, being neutral, they also have their darker side: and I know their effect upon negative minds could be very lowering. So we ask all of you who are working for the future of mankind to envelop these rays with your love, and to transmute them into a valuable growing asset for man on this planet.

"The one fact to remember above all others at this moment is that all who are awake to the perils of the hour must *think love* into this great vortex of power which is now being freed into your atmosphere.

"Your scientists will grasp its meaning and use it for all kinds of different tasks. But *you* must infuse into it the element of love, to shield the young, and those countless unawakened souls from the dangers and imbalances that now threaten the very stability of the world and its peoples."

You can imagine how much this gave us to think about. Once again, H-A's words "the secret of withdrawing the sword Excalibur" flashed through my mind.

And as for the truth of what Wellesley Tudor Pole said, that reference of his to "a scent of flowers unknown to you" really hit the button:

Because, as we had begun to climb the hill, we all stopped and sniffed. A subtle scent, unlike any flower or shrub we knew, was everywhere around us.

And yet there were no flowers or shrubs around us where we stood.

17 INTO THE FIELD

For some years before Pete added his own special skills to Operation Excalibur, my companions and I had visited certain ancient sites whenever we could—particularly at equinoxes and solstices, when somehow the energies seemed to be enhanced or multiplied.

Our aim was simple: not being dowsers or geomancers, we arrived on site, intuited the frequency of the place and then invoked healing or some similar energy, either for the planet as a whole, or for some country or region torn by war, famine or tragedy of some other kind.

Our visits were strictly of the "Thy will be done" variety.

It often occurred to us on these expeditions that we were not going about our own business but were being sent to these locations for some purpose we could only guess at. We were less knights and ladies on the chessboard than willing messengers or apprentice engineers.

Our work in the field was no concerted programme; just a group of friends with similar interests who got together whenever we could, to do our thing.

Perhaps the best way to convey the atmosphere of these adventures would be to assemble some of the highlights for you:

The south of England suffered a severe drought in the summer of 1976. Much of Devon and Cornwall was scorched and dry; fires were breaking out everywhere. Time to put our money where our mouth is, we decided.

We drove to Silbury Hill, the largest man-made hill in Europe and believed to be the site of ancient Nature rituals. Ignoring the "Keep Out" signs posted at its foot, we climbed to the top. Tony, our music man—his PA systems had relayed the sound at most of the free festivals during the 'seventies—had brought a pair of tall Caribbean drums with him.

As Tony beat out a steady, insistent rhythm, we chanted and danced like American Indians, perambulating clockwise then anticlockwise round the summit. The ceremony rose to a sort of climax, then by common consent we stopped, and flung ourselves down onto the grass, breathless and laughing.

A moment later, Tony said, "Five days."

"Yes, that's what I got!" someone else cried.

We had all received the distinct message that the drought would end in five days' time.

"Please don't send the rain all at once, and drown everything," I said, looking up at the sky. "Make it gentle and continuous for a day or two."

Five days later, as promised, the rains came—gentle, healing and persistent—and the drought was over. Whether we had affected anything with our little rain-dance, or simply picked up what was already on the cards, who knows?

The Portobello Road market in west London, one early Saturday afternoon. Thousands of visitors pack the street. Without warning it begins to rain. People run for cover, putting up umbrellas and newspapers to keep their heads dry.

I have a few heartfelt words with the Nature spirits:

"Look, fellers, this market only opens on Saturday, and people come from all over the place—even from Europe and America—to hunt for bargains. Could you hold off until half-past five—then you can rain all you like."

I know you'll trust me when I say that the rain stops immediately. Down come the umbrellas, and within seconds the street is packed again.

I walk down a side street into Ladbroke Grove, a hundred yards away. It is raining heavily. I hurry back to the Portobello. Not a drop. To double-check, I hurry back to Ladbroke Grove. Still raining.

I wait around till half-past five, just to make sure. I needn't have bothered:

On the dot, it begins to rain on the Portobello.

The next perimeter point on the Circle of Light, after Glastonbury Tor, is near Llantwit Major in south Wales. We visit it on a cold autumn day and find a small, grassy arena or amphitheatre, constructed two thousand years ago by the Roman troops garrisoned nearby.

Impulsively I run into the centre of the arena, fling my arms out and begin to whirl round, clockwise, like a Dervish.

There is an immediate growl of thunder and within seconds the rain is coming down in stair-rods.

Feeling like Mickey Mouse at the end of "The Sorcerer's Apprentice" sequence in *Fantasia*, I rush for the cover of a nearby souvenir and post-card shop and rejoin my longsuffering companions.

Three of us were standing on the guardian rock, early one autumn afternoon, when I felt a sudden blinding stab of pain in my forehead. I staggered back, sat down and tried to recover.

A few days later I heard from the wife of a young friend of mine in Plymouth whom I call "Frogg". He had taken his little son, Michael, to a swimming pool and dived off the top board to amuse him. His head struck the bottom, other swimmers noticed a cloud of blood floating from him, and life guards dived in to fish him out.

Frogg soon recovered, thank God.

I asked Julie when exactly did the accident take place?

"Saturday afternoon, at about two o'clock," she said.

The very moment I was poleaxed on that hilltop, more than a hundred miles away.

Some months later I was woken by a pain under my rib-cage that felt as if someone had stuck a red-hot screwdriver in me and was twisting it.

Later that morning, I heard that my Aunty Jo had just had a duodenal operation.

Nigel rang and asked if we could visit Ragged Stone Hill with his girlfriend, Jackie. As our car came to a halt in the hollow of White Leafed Oak, Jackie said, "Why do you keep coming here?" Her tone wasn't the least hostile, but it had an edge to it nonetheless.

I shrugged. "Because something amazing happens every

time we do, I suppose." I should point out that Jackie, who was very short-sighted, wore thick pebble-glasses which magnified things several times.

We climbed to the summit rock and, while Nigel and I shut our eyes to do the usual invocation, Jackie was content to peer out over the surrounding landscape, far below us.

Suddenly she screamed. Startled, Nigel and I opened our eyes. Standing with her glasses in one hand, Jackie was pointing in the direction of Golden Valley with the other. "Nigel, I can *see*!!"

"Fantastic," said Nigel.

"You see that field shaped like a triangle?" she said excitedly. "And that man in Wellingtons walking his dog?!"

Even Nigel and I had to squint to find the man and his dog, at least half a mile away and three or four hundred feet below. But Jackie, bless her, could see them as clearly as if they were only twenty yards away.

As we scrambled back down to the car, she kept repeating, "I can see! I can see!"

I warned her that the small miracle might only be temporary, and might have occurred to show her that some places *do* have certain powers. But Jackie was adamant; an hour later, over tea at a friend's house, nearby, she announced that she was going to see her optician next week, and order soft lenses.

She was as good as her word. Three days later she asked her optician to re-test her eyes as she wanted to start wearing soft lenses.

He smiled indulgently at her. "You? Soft lenses? With *those* eyes?!" He shook his head sadly. "Not in a hundred years."

Jackie wouldn't budge. "I want the test, and I want the lenses."

To humour her—or maybe to prove his point—the optician *did* test her eyes again. And got the shock of his life.

To this day, Jackie is wearing those lenses she had insisted on.

The pebble glasses?

I think she jumped on them.

"The current model of a man is someone who exercises his strength and ingenuity at the expense of others; who uses any means to achieve his own ends; who hides his emotions, distrusts his intuition, finds his women convenient, pliable but illogical; who shies away from anything in himself that approaches gentleness or compassion, caring or love.

"This tradition has brought civilisation to its knees. If man is to survive, he must acknowledge and welcome the feminine *within* himself."

"M"

MICHAEL DEAN

18 THE CIRCLE OF POWER

Do you remember me telling you of the dream I had, back in 1974, in which John Prudhoe took me to meet the Magician? Well, immediately after that scene faded, something else happened which I have been keeping until now:

Merlin and the anteroom vanished. In their place, an Ordnance Survey map of southern England rose up in front of me. The forefinger of some unseen person—Merlin again, I presume—traced a vertical line from Beachy Head on the south coast to the Saffron Walden area in Essex.

A voice said, "Fifty-two, fifty-two."

[A few years later, when Bob Balaban in *Close Encounters* realised that the number the spaceship had been transmitting was a map reference, my hair stood on end.]

Next morning I bought an Ordnance Survey map of south-east England. I already knew that 52 degrees latitude runs horizontally through England, passing fairly close to Ragged Stone Hill, so I traced it eastward and stopped near Saffron Walden—then looked down to the bottom of the map.

There was the figure 52 again! Representing 52,000 metres east of the nearest longitude line.

We did some research, and discovered that the exact spot we were looking for was a small wood near Audley End, a lovely Jacobean mansion which in the reign of William II had been the royal palace of England!

We visited the wood one afternoon.

It was like entering hell.

The trees were blackened and stunted, there were no grass, flowers or green vegetation. It was the kind of place where you might expect to run into demons or malignant dwarfs, cut-throats or brigands.

We found a small clearing, stood in a circle and decided to do a cleansing operation. Within seconds, a great wind blew up out of nowhere. Soon it was scouring the trees, blowing leaves and twigs and dry bracken horizontally through the air. At last it died, and the wood fell silent.

Wordlessly we left the place.

91

We picnicked in the grounds of Audley End, and John Prudhoe promised to do a little more research to find out what had prompted this strange expedition—and what had happened to cast such a dreadful spell on that wood.

He turned up trumps:

The wood is the centre of an identical circle to our beloved Circle of Light. But this one is a circle of power. Hence the royal palace at its centre. And what is more, Oxford, Norwich Cathedral and Canterbury Cathedral are situated on its perimeter!

London is contained by it.

So *this* was the wheel of power—the unseen dynamo behind Britain's rise to pre-eminence in the world, in time gone by. Whereas the Circle of Light, its counterpart and opposite, is the wheel of Britain's spiritual nature.

And why the terrible atmosphere in that wood?

Because Matthew Hopkins, Witchfinder General at the time of Cromwell, had executed countless victims there: so many, in fact, that the place still bore the scars of his terrible work.

Here, then, was a living reminder of our dark and bloody history. The history of the abuse of power. Thank God there is no Witchfinder General today, I thought, or *we'd* have his wolf-packs breathing down our necks.

And yet, a thousand years before the sinister Matthew Hopkins, it was already going on:

The ancient Roman engineers were celebrated in Britain for their straight roads. Of course: wherever possible, they built them on ley lines which acted as a power grid, sustaining Roman dominance for centuries. And later, although the Church did everything in its power to stamp out the old religion and the old beliefs in Britain, it discovered that certain ancient sites had a distinct resonance of their own, so churches were built on them. In this way the long reign of the Church, too, was powered by this invisible grid.

Viewed dispassionately from the perspective of the present day, the villainy of the Church militant in bygone days almost beggars belief. Its henchmen persecuted, tortured and murdered anyone they could find who knew anything about terrestrial and cosmic energies, who collaborated with Nature, observed her rhythms and cycles, who healed or ministered privately to the sick and the oppressed, or who worshipped older gods. During this bloody epoch, the Church claimed not thousands, but *millions* of such victims in Europe alone.

It is probably true to say that if these countless custodians of the Earth had *not* been ruthlessly culled, but had been allowed to practise their arts and pass them on to their children, we would not be facing the ecological disaster that now confronts us.

It has also been pointed out that the practice of making the sign of the cross on a person's forehead during baptism and communion is nothing more than a ritualistic method of closing that person's "third eye". If this is indeed so—and I pray that it is not—if a concerted attempt has been made to deprive entire generations of their inner sight, then another monstrous crime must be added to those already heaped at the Church door.

The litany goes on:

Take the words "heathen and "pagan", for example—used by the Church to accuse and defame. What do they really mean? I decided to find out—and what a shock was waiting for me! "Heathen" means simply "of the heath", and "pagan" means "of the countryside". How obscene that such simple, natural and innocuous words should have been corrupted by the Church for its own ends.

And what of "heresy" and "heretic", those war-cries of the Inquisition which spelt death for countless good and innocent people? "Heresy", I discovered, comes from the Greek word *"haeresis"*, meaning "choice", and "heretic" from *"haeretikos"*, meaning "able to choose"!

So, for choosing to remain faithful to their own beliefs, millions died at the hands of an institution purporting to embody the ethic of love and forgiveness! The sheer depravity of it all is enough to take one's breath away.

I have scoured the New Testament several times, but nowhere can I find any warrant or sanction for spreading the Word by means of the sword and thumb-screw. And yet, throughout what have deservedly come to be called the Dark Ages, the Church used fear, arrest, confiscation of property, interrogation, torture and murder to impose its authority.

Does that sound familiar? It should do: it reincarnated in our own century, wearing a new uniform and bearing a new name:

Gestapo.

All this, thanks be, is a hideous nightmare of the past. There are hopeful signs coming from all around the world that people will no longer allow themselves to be ground into the dust by ruthless regimes. If our refusal to be treated like ciphers ever again is the fruit of so many centuries of oppression, then all will not have been in vain.

19 OPERATION EXCALIBUR

I had frankly forgotten H-A's prophecy about groups "rediscovering the secret of extracting the sword Excalibur", when a friend of ours, Colin Bloy, an eminent dowser and geomancer, returned from the Pyrenees carrying a strange and powerful stone—the Grail stone of the Albigenses. Following some inner prompting, he had travelled to France, searched the mountain area near Rennes-le-château, and found this stone—just as his intuition told him he would.

It is the remaining half of a small circular quartz geode, containing at its heart a natural cross of white crystal. Colin believes it to be one of the sacred relics of the Cathars, a valiant band of true Christians hounded and destroyed by the Popes of Avignon, centuries ago.

I asked him if he would bring this treasure to White Leafed Oak, as we were about to make one of our seasonal pilgrimages there. Colin kindly agreed.

On the appointed afternoon we climbed the hill and took our places round the Ragged Stone—["Round the rugged rock the ragged rascals ran"!]—high above the Worcestershire plain. Colin held up the Grail stone and, to my surprise and pleasure, said:

"Withdraw the Sword, and point it in the ten directions."

We did so, first visualising Excalibur rising out of the ground, then lifting it and directing the tip of the blade, in turn, at the ten equidistant sites lying round the perimeter of the great Circle, some sixty-three miles away beyond the horizon.

We waited until we could see and feel the incandescent energy spreading throughout the British Isles like the spokes of a huge etheric wheel, then planted the sword back in the rock at our feet [the Sword in the Stone?!] and quietly left the hilltop, well satisfied with the day's work.

This was probably the first conscious move we made to set Operation Excalibur into motion. From then on, exasperated by the incessant bad news relayed daily by the media, Pete decided that we should unsheath the sword as often as time and circumstance allowed.

First, we visited the centre of the Circle of Power, near Saffron Walden; then, forty-five days later, we returned to the Malvern Hills; another forty-five days later, friends of ours in York carried out the third phase. The fourth we had to do by remote control: lack of funds prevented us from visiting the Isle of Wight, off the south coast, where Pete and Bran had once seen the tip of the sword buried.

After each phase, we sensed wave after wave of powerful, light-filled energy flowing away in every direction over Britain, as if some huge pebble had been dropped into the ethers of these islands, causing ripples to mark its entry.

In all our fieldwork, we have always been aware of the presence of one of the four Guardians: either the wisdom and deep, volcanic laughter of the Magician, or the subtle influence of the Lady; the brisk, efficient energy of the King, or the mischief and humour of the Master of Ceremonies.

Why "Operation Excalibur"? Because, as Pete once reminded me, "The sword is the emblem of the 'King' energy— the power attributed to Arthur, Saint Michael, Saint George and to Christ himself. But remember, this power is spiritual, not temporal."

This time round, Excalibur's role is to cut away the dross and illusion that have been holding us all in their thrall, and to reveal the truth. It is *not* a weapon of war, and yet some people—particularly those who are holding on to ill-gotten power, status and wealth—will feel the sharpness of its blade as acutely as if the Sword *were* being wielded in traditional combat!

20 MANITTOO!

As the 'seventies sped by, and the number of our field expeditions increased, we soon learned that it is not only in Britain and France that ancient stoneworks and circles are to be found. America has a rich sacred landscape of her own, and the spiritual sophistication of her earliest inhabitants is only now being properly recognised and acknowledged.

A good example of our discoveries is the following passage from *MANITOU—The Sacred Landscape of New England's Native Civilization*, by James W Mavor, Jr and Byron E Dix [Inner Traditions International, of Rochester, Vermont]:

By observing the natural landscape and the sky together, we were struck by the abundance and placement of earthen and stone man-made constructions, and they have communicated to us a way of life that was in harmony with Nature and we have come to believe that the Algonquian word *"manitou"* best describes this perception.

Roger Williams, one of the earliest English colonists to take a sympathetic interest in the Indians, noticed this and wrote [in his book *A Key Unto the Language of America*, London 1643]:

"Besides, there is a general Custom amongst them, at the apprehension of an Excellency in Men, Women, Birds, Beasts, Fish, etc., to cry out, 'Manittoo!' that is, 'It is a god!' as thus if they see one man excell other in Wisdom, Valour, Strength, Activity, etc., they cry out, 'Manittoo, a God!'"

How strange it is that Americans have so often said to their cousins across the Atlantic, "Oh, how we envy you your history and traditions!"

For who would dare to say that Chartres cathedral is a higher achievement than an American Indian serpent mound—or European allopathic medicine more potent than the ancient medicine of the plains?

Merlin himself once threw fresh light on American civilisation for me—in the most unexpected way:

An inveterate gamester, he loves nothing more than wordplay. It was he who, years ago, first sparked my interest in "cognate" anagrams, by showing me that if you rearrange the letters of the word "schoolmaster", you get "the classroom". I think you'll agree, they don't come any more magical than *that*.

I tried to make up a few of my own, but never got anywhere near it. The best I could manage were such pairs as:

Mimes an orchestra	[Oscar Hammerstein]
Dress in a panic	[Princess Diana]
Huge leader calls	[Charles de Gaulle]
Thin Yank person	[Anthony Perkins]
I'm no ogre	[Geronimo]
Hey! Miracles in LA!	[Shirley MacLaine]

Then one evening "M" said, "If you wish, I'll give you a brief self-portrait of America—in ten anagrams of the words 'UNITED STATES OF AMERICA'. Ready?"

I grabbed a pen and paper. "Ready," I replied. "M" cleared his throat. Then:

"One:	MEET OUR FANTASTIC IDEAS.
"Two:	MUST IT CONFEDERATE ASIA?
"Three:	I CONFIRMED A SEA STATUTE.
"Four:	ATOMIC SITE RATED UNSAFE.
"Five:	CIA STARTED TO USE FAMINE.
"Six:	i.e. SUSTAIN DEMOCRAT FATE.
"Seven:	OFTEN TRAUMATIC DISEASE.
"Eight:	SAM UNFIT TO CREATE IDEAS.
"Nine:	SENATE DIRECTS MAFIA OUT.
"Ten:	CAME TO NATURE, SATISFIED."

So there they were: eight facets of recent American history, and two possibly prophetic glimpses of her immediate future—all encapsulated in this nation's *own name*:

1: world centre of enterprise, creativity and get-up-and-go;
2: America as interventionist, policeman to the world;
3: naval power bases;
4: the Cold War and the nuclear balance of terror;
5: the Intelligence agencies as cynical chessmasters;
6: the Republican era;
7: AIDS;
8: growing foreign dissatisfaction with US muscle-flexing;
9: the phasing out of organised crime;
10: a return to Nature and sanity.

An unblinking self-appraisal by a great nation, crucible of mankind-to-be, showing the pendulum swinging from positive to negative and back to positive again—all in only 38 words!

"And how about this one to round them all off?" added the Magician. "The fate of all but the greatest movie stars: CINEMA ARTISTE FADES OUT."

"Merlin," I said, "you're too much."

I heard that laugh of his, echoing away as he left. "Aren't I just?" he replied.

The guy who could have killed Vaudeville all on his own.

And will doubtless help us rescue the world—and ourselves with it.

21 OVERTURE TO A NEW AGE

One cloudless, star-shot summer night, Pete and I were visiting friends who have a cottage near the Malvern Hills. As midnight approached, Pete slipped out into the garden and was gone for more than an hour. When he finally came back indoors, he was pale and quiet—far from his usual ebullient self. It was as if he had undergone a profound experience, emotional or otherwise, so I decided not to press him for an explanation.

Several weeks passed before he told me what had happened:

"Seven minutes past midnight into the seventh day of the seventh month of 1977, I was standing alone in that tiny Gloucestershire garden. All around me I sensed the presence of Merlin, like an awesome vortex of power. He revealed to me many aspects of the return of the Arthurian energy, the Knights of the Round Table, the future of Britain and the world. I asked to be given a tangible sign that what I was hearing was correct, and that what I was seeing was truth.

"At that moment a shooting star broke from the constellation I associate with the King.

"I wept for sheer joy, and bowed my head. The heavens were shimmering with such intensity that for an instant the garden itself was illuminated. It was a breathless moment, which no words are adequate to describe. I felt humbled, insignificant. And, as I raised my eyes again, I witnessed the beginning of the first 'note' in the cosmic overture. As the rippling shimmer of sound and light spread out across the sky, the King spoke:

"'As has long been foretold, an Arthur figure will be back among his people in their time of need. Knights and Ladies are already gathering in isolated groups, drawn together by some hidden purpose.

"'When the time is right, all the principal players will gather at a given place, known only to a few. I shall appear to them, and they will then know what they must do. Their courage must be that of lions, for at that moment there will be no room for the faint-hearted.'

"'Knights' and 'Ladies' was the language I was expecting to hear the King use at that time, but this doesn't mean that these people are elite in any way—they are simply courtesy titles for those who have dedicated themselves to serving in whatever way they can.

"The number seven has anchored us to Earth for far too long. The reason for the heavy emphasis on sevens on the day of my vision was, I believe, to point out to me the end of their sovereignty.

"The number of the future is eight. If you think in terms of music, seven notes are an incomplete octave—the eighth note finishes it, *and* starts the next. With too much emphasis on seven, one gets locked into the physical worlds. To reach the higher worlds, we must move away from seven, or we shall go round and round in circles getting nowhere."

22 SQUARING THOSE CORN CIRCLES

I recently chanced on two fragments of information that throw a most intriguing light on the mysterious "corn circles" that have been appearing throughout Wiltshire and the west country of England. The first is from an American authoress of remarkable insight and perception; the second from an old, old friend.

Elizabeth Van Buren says in *The Sign of The Dove*, quoting the Comte de Saint Germain:

"The Sword was the alchemical symbol for the act of separating the real from the illusory, the true from the false. Once the initiate has attained his inner soul balance, exemplified by *the three interlocked circles* of spirit, soul and body, and in this way has gained his sword of righteousness, he can wield this in the service of his fellow man, cutting down all obstacles which stand in the way of the progress of humanity as a whole. The soul-force of the initiate passes down the blade into the steel and blends with the power of the Creator."

She herself goes on:

"So every human being can become a Golden Man, a man of Venus. Corn was one of the grains that was brought to Earth by the gods, possibly from Venus. Corn became the symbol for gold to the alchemists, and in veiled language their sacred books depicted each grain of corn as a seed of gold or a miniature sun buried in the dense physical body of Man, ready to shine forth and transmute it completely.

"The three versions of the story of Christ in the field of corn, which form part of the secret message in the ancient documents at Rennes-le-Château, speak of the field of gold that is the potential of humanity as a whole—the millions of golden grains that can become a field of living souls, Golden Man, ready for harvesting. The harvest is almost upon us. The Great Work of the alchemists will be completed.

"Those who read these words and have understood, must act, taking up the Sword of Righteousness, and, as a soldier of the Light, fight against injustices and cruelties, against ignorance and wrong-teachings—against all that which holds mankind enslaved.

"In this way, they will be acting as the Knights of the past and their king, Arthur, Prince of Peace, who were one and all Knights of the Quest, the Quest for the Holy Grail."

And here is an extraordinary insight into all this, from a most unexpected source: King Henry VI, Part III, Act II, Scene I, by William Shakespeare:

A plain near Mortimer's Cross, Herefordshire

Edward: Dazzle mine eyes, or do I see three suns?

Richard: Three glorious suns, each a perfect sun,
not separated with the racking clouds,
But sever'd in a pale clear-shining sky.
See, See! they join, embrace and seem to kiss,
As if they vowed some league inviolable:
Now they are one lamp, one light, one sun,
In this the heavens figure some event.

Edward: 'Tis wondrous strange, the like yet never
heard of. I think it cites us, brother to the field,
That we the sons of brave Plantagenet
Each one already blazing by our meeds,
Should not withstanding join our lights together
And over-shine the earth as this the world.
Whate'er it bodes, henceforward will I bear
Upon my target three fair-shining suns...

Herefordshire! Is there *no* limit to the mystery and magic of the Malverns and their surrounding countryside?! Apparently not.

In any event, it seems that, since earliest times, our "friends in high places" have been dropping as many hints as they dare—and are now, with increasing urgency and frequency, guiding us towards the coming age, *and* providing us with a compass as we go. All *we* have to do is recognise the oh-so-eloquent writing on the wall!

23 THINGS TO COME?

One evening, after supper in the cottage, we decided to do a short visualisation exercise in turn, then tell what we had seen. Bran found herself in a landscape of indescribably lovely colours and sounds; Pete saw Merlin juggling with what looked like planets and suns. Eventually it was my go.

"Come on," challenged Pete, "let's see what *you* get."

For some reason I felt unusually confident and knelt down. "Fasten your seatbelts, boys and girls," I said with rather reckless self- assurance. "This is going to be a barn-burner!"

Everyone smiled indulgently.

I closed my eyes. Almost at once a chalice made of light floated towards me out of the darkness. I put out both hands, placed it reverently on the ground in front of me and lowered my forehead to the carpet.

Now a sword floated towards me, hilt first. For a few moments I held it horizontally on my palms, then grasped the hilt and raised the blade until it touched my brow. Then I held the sword at arm's length, point uppermost. For a moment it glowed blue, then in an instant it turned into incandescent *energy* and sped away like a shooting star to the Draco constellation in the northern night sky. [Don't ask me how I knew that—the knowledge was automatic and instantaneous, as it so often is with these things.]

I bowed low, my forehead touched the ground again, and I concentrated deeply. A moment or two later the darkness began to lighten and I saw a huge faceted crystal, buried deep in the earth. I straightened up and, eyes still closed, peered far into the air directly above me.

It was unmistakable: a solitary star, shining steadily in the night sky. Again I peered down at the crystal, then up at the lone star. Gradually I became aware of a faint column of light— the faintest silvery-blue etheric glow—joining star to crystal.

"This is a new covenant for the coming Age," I heard myself announce. "A precious bond between Earth and her new Pole star, which will appear over the new North Pole after the changes."

Well, you can make of that what you will—but before you do make up your mind one way or the other, here is the sequel:

About a month later, Pete, James and I drove to Golden Valley, at the foot of our favourite range of hills. We arrived at dusk, and were drawn to one particular field where two folds in the ground made the shape of an immense sword. Pete stood for a while at the hilt of this "sword", then called me over and asked what I could pick up.

I knelt down, lowered my forehead to the grass and concentrated. At once the crystal reappeared—a huge chunk of translucent quartz, I think, and roughly faceted.

I opened my eyes and looked up into the darkening sky. My heart missed a beat—there was the solitary star, directly above us!

"Good God!" I exclaimed. The vision in Pete's sitting room had come to life!

For a full twenty minutes—it was quite dark by now—no other star appeared. We walked back to the car, only a hundred yards away, and as we drove off, took a last look at the sky.

All the stars were out now!

Later Peter did some research and found out that our lone star was Vega. A day or so after this, his investigations led him to an article that mentions a very strong candidate for the new Pole star, after "the changes":

Vega!

I've long since ceased to be amazed by Merlin's sky-writing, but making *all* the stars disappear?!

And how about this:

Once, we took a friend, Edward Posey, to Ragged Stone. It was a cloudless day, but while we were doing our invocation, John Prudhoe and I noticed that a solitary cloud had appeared, directly above us. It was a perfect caricature of Edward, right down to his Phoenician nose and jutting grey beard. John had the presence of mind to whip out his camera, so we have proof of the Magician's sense of humour.

And Pete himself is no slouch: once, while we were standing on the guardian rock, I tried to swat an importunate bee; Pete scolded me, called the bee back, then asked it to settle on his outstretched finger. The bee did so. Pete then asked it to land on Bran's finger. It did. And so on, round the group. Finally, Pete asked me to apologise to the creature, and it *might* do the same again. I did—and after circling me warily three times, the bee alighted on my hand.

A few summers ago, a number of us took a small cottage on the island of Iona, off the western coast of Scotland. Every morning after breakfast, we split up and went our own ways, returning early in the evening to exchange our news.

One afternoon I walked to "the bay at the back of the ocean", as the map calls it. As I approached the wide, deserted shoreline, an ominous black pall of cloud, hanging over the sea like a shroud, headed straight for me. Normally when this happens, I run for cover. This time, for some reason, I opened my arms and shouted, "Welcome!"

The storm blew in over me and, to my surprise, instead of being lashed by chilly rain and wind, I felt as if I was in a warm and loving embrace.

A day or so later, sitting high on the moor in the stillness and fitful sunlight—and wondering how much *more* pain and suffering must be endured before we wake from our self-induced nightmare—I half-closed my eyes.

Within seconds the moorland had gone and I was in some other place altogether, lit by an incandescent sun. People, hundreds of them, radiant, untroubled, were gathered for some ceremony or other on a hillside. I heard music of a kind I have never heard before, laughter and birdsong.

A feeling of inexpressible relief came over me. Something was telling me that this was not a glimpse of the distant past, nor mere imagination, but from the future.

"How far in the future?" I asked.

"That, as ever, is up to you," came the immediate reply.

5. INITIATIONS

"The Earth herself is about to undergo the latest of a number of initiations. Much has been spoken of these coming changes, which, from our perspective, can only be seen as a cleansing, and can only lead to a more enlightened age. Are *you* ready for these changes?"

"M"

24 FACETS OF MYSELF

In ancient Egypt, students of the mysteries would be taught by priests and priestesses and undergo a series of initiations in the temple. Elsewhere, they would attend one of the mystery schools. Nowadays, as these forms of instruction are seldom available, many of our tests and initiations take place on the inner planes—during sleep, as often as not. Here is a notable example, described by Roy Davis, a friend who lives near the Malverns:

I was planning to do a vibe on Ragged Stone hill to welcome the spring equinox, but something happened before my proposed visit to change that. In fact, it made my visit quite unnecessary.

The night before, I had a dream like none I have ever had, before or since. It was so real, it's as if it only happened a few minutes ago, and in such detail that I couldn't hope to record it all here—but here is the gist of it:

My presence was required by three very powerful, compassionate and—how can I describe it?—infinitely adult beings. They sought me specifically, when as far as I was aware, they had no way of knowing I even existed.

There was never any question in my suddenly very calm and peaceful mind that I should do exactly as they asked. They appeared as two men and a woman, all apparently in their prime. No words were spoken, although I was instructed and reassured telepathically throughout our contact.

Two of these beings emitted lights, with colours of indescribable purity, and from different angles these lights were projected at me. They travelled slowly enough for me to see the beams reach out and focus in/on me. Whereupon a kind of physical and emotional hologram sprang to life inside me—actively! Senses and feelings swept through me that seemed infinitely more real than any I have ever had.

This stopped after a while and a "search" began. They wanted to "locate" me somewhere on a scale of being. Now the woman directed my attention to a row of crystal objects, identical but for differences too subtle for me to determine. Her message was that I should give them my effort in what was about to happen, but I would remain calm and not resistant. I was protected.

Unquestioningly I accepted this.

She pointed at each crystal from left to right, very quickly. I felt strange for an instant.

"Now, be calm," was the instruction she gave me as she pointed at each crystal in turn, slowly this time.

Nothing happened as she pointed at the first few, then suddenly, as she moved to the next one, my whole being was seized by an emotional earthquake. My greatest hopes, worst fears, love, hate, compassion, dread, longing, loathing—all flooded through me with urgent, explosive power.

Everything I ever was or could ever be, happened all at once! It was real and it was terrifying, and in the part of me they spoke to, I sensed that they had *really found—me*!

It ended with me as calm and untroubled as I had been before—though I could somehow see myself white-faced and sweat-drenched with an exertion I hadn't even felt.

They were pleased with me without overtly expressing their thanks. "And now," they seemed to say, "you shall have your rock, and an understanding for your efforts."

And guess where I found myself transported to in an instant? Yes, Ragged Stone! As I stood on top of the guardian rock my awareness grew stronger, sharper and more penetrating than before. And I came to understand some natural relationships that I wasn't even aware existed before. I felt my own physical structure change like, well, like facets appearing on a growing crystal.

And that was it.

So you can see why I didn't feel I needed to visit Ragged Stone. After all, I'd already been there!

25 GIFTS FROM THE MAGE

A dear friend of ours, Evelyn Winn, was told by her physician that she must undergo major surgery without delay. She was admitted to hospital and prepared for the operation. As the anaesthetic began to take effect, she found herself embarking on "one of the strangest and most beautiful experiences of my life":

I was floating away from the hospital on a kind of cloud-bed. It was as if I was wrapped in cottonwool. I was immersed in it and just drifting along. The colours around me were indescribable, a kind of iridescent pink shot through with subtle blues and mauves. I couldn't see anyone around me, but I sensed companions gently escorting me.

We went into a very bright place, where I became aware of a brilliant globe. We went right into it and the light became intense and blinding. Now I found myself in a room. Its sides were of every conceivable colour, from palest pink right through the spectrum. The eight walls were paneled or faceted, though it is difficult to be precise about them as they appeared to be flowing into each other.

I felt my companions massaging my brow and stroking my head. Then they removed a layer of the 'cottonwool' and I was able to move around in the cocoon a little more easily.

Suddenly a quiet, majestic voice spoke to me. I somehow knew it was Merlin:

"Well, Mother, at last we meet. I shall not show myself to you for the moment, as your concept of me is far nicer than anything I could conjure up! I shall not disillusion you.

"You had to have this operation. You only really begin to appreciate the physical life when every single experience is undertaken personally. Being close to death has a centering effect: this is necessary as it will enable you to progress further along the Path.

"I am soon going to take you on a journey through light and sound. Although they may seem at first to be merely flashes and noises, each one will mean something to you. But first I

112

will let you sleep."

A blissful sensation of peace and weightlessness came over me. A cool feeling began at my feet and spread up to my head, and I drifted off into a fathomless sleep.

When I awoke I was sitting up in the 'cloud', looking out over a vast green valley. I was aware of every conceivable shade of green there. Eventually, Merlin spoke:

"Your operation has been successful. Your emotions and sensations will now be more highly tuned. Remember that one of the prime reasons you are where you are, in the physical world, is to dispel other people's fears and illusions."

I replied that I felt that this task was rather difficult, because it would be impossible to love everybody all the time, and I didn't feel qualified to do this.

Merlin gestured around us. "This will help you to under-stand yourself a little better. You are what you are for a pur-pose—humble, without pretensions yet with great good sense. It is necessary to give someone a 'smack in the mouth' at times—you understand this, do you not? Then again, you have to pick them up and dry their tears, and this too is part of your function. Do not always assume that you are going to fail before you start!"

We then went for a stroll together into the valley. We passed through a brightly-coloured arch, then stopped on the shore of a vast lake. The sand was pure white and the lake a shimmering mirror-blue.

Merlin put me into a boat. It was a strange misty craft, long and thin yet oddly indistinct and insubstantial. We drifted away from the shore. Merlin told me that he was going to give me something very precious. They were not to be used directly by me, but would be used by others who came to me.

In the middle of the lake another golden-white orb appeared, and we sailed right into it. I found myself in a glitter-ing crystal cave of every imaginable colour. When I ceased gaz-ing around in wonder, I realised that I was holding a huge purple crystal crowned by a luminous blue five-pointed star. And laid across my knees was an enormous sword—massive, yet weightless.

Merlin told me to take these gifts back and present them to those for whom they were intended. And I should not shirk my duty as "chairwoman" any longer.

"Remember, Mother, when the warrior-King, the mystic-Magician and the Lady meet, there must you stand to advise. The Magician will use these tools to unlock the knowledge you are about to be given. You cannot unlock it yourself."

An orangy-yellow haze formed round me and I was laid back in a room of many mirrors. Merlin whispered that he would visit me often and impart various aspects of knowledge:

"These things you will remember when the time is right—when the warrior and mystic need them."

The next thing I remember is recovering from the anaesthetic and being back in the ward. It was a wonderful experience, and has given me great faith and hope for the future.

MICHAEL DEAN

26 INTO THE SUN

"Look within," Merlin told us on more than one occasion. "Be your own launch pad and your own space probe."

And so, as the 1970s progressed, the ancient art of mind travel, practised so long ago in Egypt, Tibet and India by adepts and students of the mysteries, resurfaced on both sides of the Atlantic. [I suspect that much of the imagery of *Close Encounters* came from Spielberg's inner, rather than outer, research.]

It enables the traveller, while still awake but in a state of deep relaxation—brainwaves at alpha—to move at will through space and time, unhampered by the limitations of normal consciousness and physical travel; to explore the boundless inner landscapes that are always there, waiting for us.

During these years, many of us, American and British explorers alike, set out on our first inner journeys. Most of our travels were monitored by an experienced 'navigator' or 'ground control' and were taped, for subsequent study and analysis.

The results were astonishing. We journeyed back through time to witness moments of history being made [no wonder the Inquisition labeled activities like this the 'black arts', punishable by death—every infamy perpetrated by Church and State was open to full inspection!]; we reviewed crucial events in our previous lives; we penetrated the Earth, investigated the deepest oceans, entered subatomic realms; we found new knowledge suddenly and effortlessly being revealed to us; we moved through space/time corridors to other planets and rose to other dimensions altogether. We even saw glimpses of the future.

The following is part of a journey I took with the help of an American friend, Joyce Petschek, who is, among her many other gifts, a highly-skilled co-pilot/navigator.

She drew the curtains in her opulent drawing-room in Ladbroke Crescent. I lay on a huge divan with a cloth over my eyes to keep out the light, and Joyce sat on the floor beside me with a small tape-recorder.

"J" is Joyce, "M" is myself:

J : What comes to you?
M : A golden eye.
J : Fine. Large or small?
M : Like the Sun. And its iris has become a tunnel.
J : Are you in the tunnel now?
M : Approaching it. It curves away to the left.
J : Is there any colour in the tunnel? Is it indigo?
M : It's dark, but there's a sort of golden colour about.
J : And how are you moving through the tunnel?
M : Flying. It's gone up into a bigger planet like an orange.
J : You've come out into an orange planet, is that it?
M : The tunnel's gone up into this planet and gone through its side.
J : Do you know what planet it is?
M : No. But I get the feeling it's the Sun.
J : Yes, it feels like the Sun. Ask what goes on up there.
M : I get an image of the surface of this world, and I've gone through the surface. But after a certain amount of time—or space, should I say?!—there's an inner planet inside it, which I haven't penetrated.
J : See if you can go into the inner planet, the inner civilisation of the Sun.
M : I'm in a purple hall.
J : Yes?
M : Very, very tall, limitless, no ceiling. It's opening out, and in the middle there's a city.
J : Yes. Go into the city.
M : Very pointed spires or something. And it's floating—it's on a column of light, like a fairytale city in a fairytale.
J : Get closer to the city and explore it.
M : Everything radiates from a central point—circles like ripples going out and out and out from the centre.
J : And what city is this?
M : I don't know.

116

J : Are there people or beings in this city?

M : Presences rather than beings.

J : And what is their function here?

M : As you asked the question, I saw an imposing back view of a judge—but I get the feeling it's a kind of benevolent eye that's watching the Solar System.

J : Ask if the judge will turn round and face you.

M : He would rather not. I think it's a case of my not being ready to see him, rather than his not being ready to see me!

J : Is there a message he wishes to impart to you?

M : I get the image of great hawk lifting its wings, which are dark purple, dark green and magenta. They lift right up above his head, as if to say, "This aspect of the Sun concerns you. He says Horus sees all, hears all, and reports to him. The hawk is the cross.

J : Is that the cross of enlightenment or the cross to bear? Or the cross of pathways?

M : It is the cross of illumination. The upright piece lit up as you asked. All the Avatars visiting the Earth have to stand in front of this cross of illumination, and only if they match its radiance…it's like a test for them before they choose themselves, consider themselves fit for their work as pathfinders.

J : This cross of illumination, how is it connected to the White Brotherhood?

M : The White Brotherhood are its rickshaw men. They are the means, humble and invisible, whereby apparently more important personages may go about doing their work. But the humble rickshaw men are, in fact, the Brotherhood that make it possible.

J : And when someone has stood before the cross and been passed by it, where does he go from there?

M : He becomes…the cross flowers in him and he becomes a transformer of its energy, which shows itself in a way that can be felt and seen and under-

117

stood by men.

J : And Horus is the keeper of this cross?

M : He is the means whereby its energy can reach us all.

J : He is the transformer of the energy?

M : The chief transformer. And there are lesser ones Some of them have been Pharaohs. I see a blue and gold figure.

J : So the Horus energy has flowed into many beings on Earth?

M : Like a waterfall over a series of rocks going down a long fall into the river.

J : And what determines whether a person goes under the Horus ray?

M : His credentials in the big computer.

J : What tests will he have had to pass?

M : Ordeal by fire—the mastery of will; ordeal by water—the mastery of emotion; ordeal by air— mastery of mind; ordeal by Earth—mastery of physical life.

J : Is Horus a being who could have left the Earth but chose to return here?

M : He is a Principle, which can in part manifest as an energy, which can in turn subdivide into exalted incarnate beings. He begins with the Trinity. He *is* the triangle, he's part of the triangle—one aspect of it. The triangle being a prime aspect of God manifest.

J : Then what dimension does the triangle oversee?

M : Fourth, fifth, sixth. Seventh dimension. Eight is another story!

I have thought a great deal about what I saw and experienced during these inner travels, and have listened to the resulting tapes several times.

I am now as sure as one can be about anything that they are *not* mental fabrications or fantasies, but actual experiences undergone by a part of the mind or one of our other subtle bodies. Just before we set off, Joyce would always say, "Don't play your *own* mind-tapes—wait until they show *you* something."

What impressed me most was the way new knowledge and information came instantly, effortlessly to mind; to say nothing of all the insights into areas we would otherwise be unlikely to encounter—glimpses of submarine and stratospheric life, for example; atomic and subatomic structures; the hidden powers of the Earth; the function of crystals, gems, metals, flowers, soil, seas; access to other times, other lives, other planets, planes and dimensions.

And their prime advantage over dreams and hypnosis alike is that one is quite conscious—and in verbal contact with one's navigator—throughout the journey.

If nothing else, these experiences have taught me in no uncertain manner that we are *not* Earthworms, confined to the ground, but skywalkers and dimension-jumpers. Having travelled several times at unimaginable speeds through space and time, in some kind of capsule or craft of etheric light, I think I now understand a little more about some of the many kinds of so-called 'flying saucers' that have been mystifying us for the past half-century.

What a pathetic reflection of our lower nature that Intelligence agencies should only think of harnessing these travelling techniques to espionage and other dirty tricks! Ah well, as the Chinese sage once said, "Why talk of the ocean to well-frogs?"

Just one other thought: Horus—the hawk. Merlin's very own trademark, once again! It makes me think that his wingspan exceeds anything we can envisage.

And how *about* that "big computer"?!

27 RETURN TO AVALON

The following is a fragment of the transcript of one of the extraordinary inner journeys made by John Prudhoe during 1976 and 1977, with Joyce Petschek once again serving as navigator. As they both have the initials JP, "N" is Joyce—the navigator, and "J" is John:

N : Tell me when the first image appears, no matter what it is.

J : There's a large library with a central dome, like an academy of life—twin gables on either side of this dome. I'm being pulled in...Wooden stairs, solid wooden balustrade inside wide entrance, but someone guarding the doors—a strong defensive and protective energy. Not everyone can get past this energy to read these books or whatever is kept here.

N : Ask if your own records are here and, if so, may we look at them?

J : Someone has a book in his hand—but he has no hand! This is strange! No hand! No face either, come to that. I have just climbed up onto a shelf; the books are huge and I feel tiny. I'm bringing down a book. *My* book. Now I'm being ushered to a table by a white-haired, wizened old monk, and I'm sitting down with the book in front of me. I feel smaller and smaller, as if I'm shrinking all the time—it's weird—but nothing else is changing size, not my body or the place I'm in; it's just this funny feeling of accelerated reversed time. Wait a minute —I have been here before. It's the Hall of the Akashic Record! The cosmic library. Yes, now I recognise the place. Wow!

N : Are you to read the book?

J : Yes, I'm told I'm allowed to look at the book. It's massive, thick, heavy and, as I open it, the pages... there *are* no pages—the book is hollow!

120

N : What can you see now?

J : I see many armed horsemen, a shield, a red shield, a man on a horse. There is a cross on the shield. It is myself on the horse, and the shield has a circle with a cross inside it. Armed men on foot are marching behind us. We are all tired.

N : Who is this man?

J : A knight.

N : And where are we?

J : France... Aquitaine. We are here to meet a lady, a most important person. We are riding homeward from the land you now call Germany. We have been travelling four days and three nights from Lower Saxony without much rest, but we are in good spirits. We are travelling homeward to the Other Isle with our ancient relics—three lances and other sacred items. We journey to Avalon.

[pause]

The Knight is riding with many others. The lances are held erect, not forward as when going into battle or coming from battle. We travel in peace, having rescued the lances.

N : What is the purpose of this Knight?

J : He is an emissary. The two outriders flanking him lead the entire column.

N : Is each of them holding a lance?

J : Yes, three lances—and there is something else being carried, but hidden from sight. It is a magical jewel.

N : What is the jewel, and the spears?

J : These are for Merlinus, gifts for the Master. We are taking them to his court on the Other Isle.

N : Which Isle?

J : The White Isles...The fair and beautiful land across the sea, the ancient isles you now call Britain.

N : Who is the Master these gifts are being returned to?

J : Ar-Tor, the leader of Ambrosius's court.

N : And the time?

J : After Christus. Our faith is older than the Christian, however, for the sacred cross within the circle is the older religion. You call us pagan, but we are not pagan. Our rites and powers descend from the Chaldeans, the masters of time and space. We are reborn Egyptians living in the Christian era—this is merely the ever-changing cycle of manifestation of the same one Truth, which is far older than Christianity.
[pause]
The cloaks change, the wind changes direction, the seasons revolve, human consciousness evolves—all things grow, they move to higher, more rarefied vibrations, atom by atom, day by day, step by step. Other forms come and go like waves on the ocean, but the inner Being never changes.

N : Where are you now?

J : The column is approaching the gates of a large city. A crowd of happy people have come out to greet the travelling party of knights and foot-soldiers.

N : Can you describe this city?

J : Yes. It's in a swamp. The people are very poor, they eat fish. And there is a peninsula which rises inland. The name Cornwall is coming forward. It is on one edge of Avalon—a far side of Avalon, a province. The purpose of rescuing the spears is to allow the Master to execute a plan of campaign. But it is one which is doomed to failure, for Ar-Tor is young and foolhardy—the young Bear who will neither be tamed nor take the wise counsel of those around him. Yet...

N : How old is Ar-Tor at this time?

J : Twenty-four.

N : What are those around him counselling?

J : To stem his eagerness for power. To wait. He is young and thinks there is nothing else he needs to know—but he has not yet been fully initiated; he is still a child of time. Some close to him seek their

122

own glory and attach themselves to him, hoping for an easy ride to power through his gullibility.

N : And where is Merlin now?

J : On his way from the lands to the north, the country of the singing fathers. You call it Wales. Oh, I see...

N : What do you see?

J : Ar-Tor will not wait. He is angry that Lord Merlin has not arrived, but Merlin has been held back by a storm at sea. Ar-Tor does not appreciate this fact. "Why does not Merlin subdue the sea?" he protests. "It is well within his power!" And yet I sense Merlin is deliberately letting things take their course and not intervening: he is testing Ar-Tor, trying to teach him tolerance and patience.

N : Do you recognise any of the other knights, or anyone else in the company?

J : Not all the knights in the group are good men. There are only a few who know the Truth and are truthful.

N : How many knights are there?

J : In all, forty or fifty, of whom a few are themselves initiates of the ancient order.

N : How many initiates are there?

J : Eight or nine. But they are not all knights—only four or five are knights.

N : Are you one of the eight or nine?

J : Yes.

N : And what is happening now?

J : The ground is receding away as I rise high above the Earth, spiralling... Yes, the Round Tables are in fact spirals of energy with stations, or human roles to be enacted at each point of the evolutionary spiral.

A number of us are rising into the finer energies, the subtler spheres and dimensions of being. In this time period there are other groups of Initiates of other temples and other planets who, from time to time, appear as human beings in the moving

123

scenario of Ar-Tor's court.

Sometimes identities are exchanged, as the group oversoul plays endless intricate games of gaining different experiences through different bodies—for instance, a knight in one life, a peasant in another; a merchant in one, a wandering minstrel in another; one life enjoying success, the next the balancing experience of poverty or failure or whatever. All is flowing, change is the one constant, 'tis true. One learns acceptance and slowly, painfully grows into detachment from the life of one's physical form. We are rising higher now...

N : What is below you?

J : Clear blue space and, below a long ways, receding away, is planet Earth.

N : And tell me what is before you.

J : We are aboard a craft, a vehicle of light. Here we are no longer wearing armour, we are wearing white robes. There are rays. It is very peaceful, placid; time is emptying itself and vibrations are clearing. Colours are purer and strengthen one's being here more than on Earth which is, in comparison and by necessary construction, duller. Few travellers could consciously bear these powerful rays at this overwhelming level.

N : How many are accompanying you?

J : A crew of extraterrestrial beings fully conscious of their functions, and ourselves, and three hermits and brothers.

N : Including Ar-Tor?

J : No. He is where he belongs, learning the ways of the Earth plane at first hand. We are now many light years away from that period of time. It is but a second in the cosmic clock; that epoch is no more than a grain of sand on an endless shore, totally irrelevant in view of the whole pattern of the cosmos, yet specially important purely because it *is*, and is part of the whole...

N : What appears before you now?

J : Asteroid belts. The Milky Way.

N : Go towards it.

J : There is a beautiful woman among our group here. She is very good...A golden energy. Very wise, very pure and beautiful soul.

N : And do you know who she is?

J : Indeed so.

N : And what is her name?

J : She is a daughter of the Sun. I cannot divulge her name, it is a word of power, great power.

N : Is she Ar-Tor's wife?

J : No. She is his guiding light and love, his guide, though he knows it not... *She* is the real figure behind Ar-Tor. Rather than Ar-Tor leading the people, *she* was the spiritual leader!

N : See where she wishes to take you.

J : To the gate, the golden gate. We stage through Alcania, fourth dimension going through to five. Sunshine and sunbeams, we're travelling through sunbeams, a carpet of them.

N : You are going through the light barrier now?

J : Correct. Angular transitional pattern.

N : Proceed, follow the guides.

J : The ship is going through energy displacement changes and raybeam alignment. Subtle interference patterns. The Earth plane equivalent would be asteroid and gamma wave bombardment. They use that as a protective circuit to change the vibrations of things entering their spheres here, like a safety net around the light barrier.

N : So you are on a spaceship now?

J : A vehicle of etheric light, yes.

N : Is this craft guiding you through to your destination?

J : The craft acts as a vehicle and a necessary protection. The crew and certain crystal-oriented mecha-

125

nisms assist in navigation, using rays. And the guide beings actually pull us through by their continuous conscious projections of thought, locked in with the crystal.

N : Is the lady with you, or has she left you?

J : She is still here. This is her place, alongside her kin.

N : Can you describe your principal guide?

J : A very peaceful being of Light.

N : And his dress?

J : He is pure light. Wears a cape of rainbowed iridescent light, mainly deep royal blue, resonant and richly mysterious, like a veil to his real nature. The cape shimmers, and has designs around its hem. These are constantly changing symbols—multidimensional cuneiform images. I can't focus them easily, they change so rapidly into something else as soon as I focus on them. In my peripheral vision they look static, but when I concentrate on them directly, they move about. He isn't of human form. He radiates love, and protects us and is taking us through these spaces. Merlin works with him, I'm being told...

I find this tantalising insight into Arthurian times quite extraordinary. It has the "right" feeling about it. It reveals what we have always suspected—that the *real* story of Merlin, Arthur and the Knights of the Round Table is probably far more magical, mysterious and mind-blowing than even legend would have us believe.

And as if that weren't enough, for some years I have had a growing impression that the saga is about to be re-enacted—on a scale so large that it is almost unimaginable...

28 THE CHALICE

During my second journey, I saw glimpses of three of my previous lives. The third of them was the following—which echoes John's Prudhoe's *Return to Avalon*—before it lifted off into higher worlds!

I should point out that John and I didn't discuss our inner journeys until several years later. There was no way we could influence or even subconsciously "borrow" from each other's transmissions.

As before, "J" is Joyce, and "M" is myself:

M : ...Again the scene has changed. Now I am aboard an Elizabethan merchant ship that has been converted into a man-of-war. Don't ask me how I know this, but I do. The vessel is flying a white flag with a red cross.

J : Why are you aboard this ship?

M : We're carrying something very precious below decks.

J : Go below then.

M : I'm in the captain's quarters. There's a small iron-bound oak chest. It's locked.

J : Open it.

M : The lid swung open the moment I touched it. There's something bulky wrapped in pale grey silk with a *fleur-de-lys* pattern woven into it.

J : So take a look.

M : It's a holy Cup, a magnificent gold chalice studded with rubies, diamonds and emeralds.

J : Why is it on the ship? Whose is it?

M : It belonged to the princes of the Church.

J : Why are you confiscating it?

M : It is the symbol of our *inner* wealth, which the Church has managed to convert into its own material wealth. Did the Founder tell his followers to collect gold and precious jewels, paid for by the pennies of the poor?

J   : Where are you taking it?

M : To England.

J   : And who are you?

M : *[proudly]* We are the Knights of the Cross, madam…

"Until you can face yourselves, and see yourselves for what and who you really are; and until you acknowledge your immense debt to the lovely planetary being who is carrying you across the celestial ocean, there can be no going forward."

"M"

6. TOWARDS THE GRAIL

29 JUST FOR THE RECORD

Now that the pieces of the jigsaw puzzle are beginning to fall into place, it no longer surprises me that the legend of King Arthur and the knights and ladies of the Round Table is one of the most enduring of all time. It has captured the imagination of many generations, and obstinately refuses to die. But the story has been told and retold so many times that, as in an old oil painting, its true colours are in danger of disappearing behind successive layers of romantic varnish.

As I have already said, I believe that this brief moment in our history was both grimmer *and* more magical than even Malory, T H White, Catherine Christian, Mary Stewart and Marion Bradley have depicted it—enthralling though each of their versions has been in its own way.

Also, as I have come to believe that the key to the future lies somewhere in the distant past, I decided that this account of my adventures with Merlin would be incomplete if I didn't ask him to cast his mind back to his time as mentor to Arthur, and beyond. After all, who better to consult than the prime mover and shaker himself!

Pete agreed to bring "M" through for me. He asked me not to show him my questions beforehand, so that he had no foreknowledge of them. In this way he would have no opportunity to colour the answers he would be channeling, even subconsciously.

I must apologise if I have failed to ask any important questions that immediately occur to you. Doubtless we shall have the chance to speak with "M" again in due course, when we can ask about some of the many things I have missed here.

The following is a transcript of the dialogue which took place in my London apartment during the spring of 1985—while outside, passenger planes came in to land at Heathrow, doors slammed, car break-in alarms went off, and a neighbouring carpenter cut a length of obstinate chipboard down to size!

"M" is Merlin, "m" is myself:

131

M : Welcome, welcome, thrice welcome. Ask your questions if you please.

m : First, thank you very much for coming, and agreeing to throw some light on our history. When you were here in the sixth century as Merlin, who were your parents?

M : I was not incarnate as you know it. I simply materialised.

m : At will?

M : *[a nod]* As different people. As different energies. As different influences. Many magical figures have appeared throughout your history, most of whom were, I must confess, aspects of me!

m : You've just pulled the rug from under my first ten questions! I was going to ask if you were lonely as a youth? Who were your special friends? Were you aware of your destiny? etcetera. And all that is now irrelevant!

M : Precisely.

m : I intended to ask who was your first teacher, and who was the Archmage of Britain at the time. Was there such a person?

M : *[indicates himself]* The Archmage is but a facet of the energy emanating from the Circle of Magicians.

m : I see. Was Arthur born at Tintagel Castle?

M : No.

m : Was he the son of the Duchess of Cornwall?

M : No.

m : Can you give some clue as to his birth and origins?

M : There have been *many* Arthurs, many figures. Where the Arthur has been, there have I been also. The Arthur is a manifesation of the "king" energy, as you have come to call it.

m : Have the Arthurian legends, then, gathered round several people who——?

M : Yes!

m : Several Arthurs?

132

M : Indeed.

m : There was not *one* called "Artor"?

M : Many! Many. It is a rank, like "the Merlin", "the King", "the President".

[a loud banging starts outside the window]

m : Excuse the noise.

M : We bring all kinds of manifestations in our wake—most of them noisy!

m : Have the Arthurs all been good pupils?

M : Impetuous sometimes, foolhardy often, but ultimately true to the Light.

m : Was there a person, Morgan Le Fay? Or does she too represent——?

M : Oh yes, oh yes. A lovely lady. Always you notice the essence of the Lady—that is, the counterpart of the Circle of Magicians, a beautiful and wonderful group of energies that has been much maligned. Morgan represents a corporate circle of "Ladies".

m : I see. And was Morgan working closely with you?

M : Where I was, she was.

m : Was Guinevere one of the circle?

M : No.

m : Was there a Guinevere?

M : No! Guinevere is a delightful touch of *broderie française*, tacked on later.

m : And Lancelot?

M : French romances!

m : Was life for the people of the 6th century in these islands a tough affair?

M : Bloody beyond belief.

m : Was there a sword Excalibur? Or does it represent something non-physical?

M : It is a symbol of the power of the spirit, the fire that burns within. In every man and woman is the shape of the sword.

m : Are there many major distortions in the Arthurian

legends that you would like to correct?

M : Many, far too many! Around the mythos have have grown countless distortions. But rather than destroy the whole, we keep to what has become accepted, as even this carries the seed within it.

m : Were you personally involved in the design and building of Stonehenge and the network of power centres throughout Britain? Or did you inspire their builders?

M : I was involved.

m : When was Stonehenge built?

M : Far earlier than you suppose. Stonehenge, or... *[pause]* Yes, it is difficult, that name will suffice to identify it, but it does not resonate to that name. That is one reason why it no longer works, why it will not function correctly. These are words of power. One day the proper word will re-emerge, and then the henge—despite the vandalism it has suffered—will function once again. It is a beacon. A key component of Earth's subtle circuitry.

m : Did the builders of the Great Pyramid in Egypt use sonics or some other method to make the stone weightless?

M : Sonics, and also the human voice.

m : The human *voice*?! Wow. And Stonehenge?

M : Stonehenge was created on the inner planes then translated into physical form. At the right moment, the stones were called out of the ethers during a ceremony of materialisation. A great celebration followed.

m : You have said you are a member of the Circle of Magicians. Could you put a name to some of your colleagues in this circle?

M : Why limit the limitless? We are notes in a cosmic octave. But each note is itself a multitude of octaves of different frequencies, and when we sing together the Universe resounds to our song.

[a pause, while the questioner considers this information!]

m : It's clear that you have returned. Has Arthur also returned?
M : I never left! You simply lost sight of me.
m : Then is "the Once and Future King", latest in the line of Arthurs, with us, physically, now?
M : There will be many Arthurs. Their influence will be great and small. You will find that within you and your companions there is an Arthur to be found.
m : Could this be said of every man?
M : To a lesser or a greater extent.
m : Could it be said of every woman that within her is potentially a Queen and an Empress?
M : Indeed.
m : And within some, a Magician?
M : Why not?
m : And in others, a Master of Ceremonies?
M : That too.
m : And that we should try to reflect *all* these archetypes within us?
M : Yet more questions whose answers you already know!
m : What is the Grail?
M : It is the hard-won wisdom and perfection that, once attained, confronts us with our own divinity. It is the state of perfect grace and equilibrium. It is the many and the One. The fountainhead. Alpha and Omega, and whatever lies between. In order to climb a mountain, you may have to descend into an unexpected crevasse or ravine before regaining the far slope. It is the journey's end—and the beginning of true service.

Anyone who thinks of the Grail as some remote myth or ideal is clearly not yet ready to devote the effort and to embody the discipline that the Quest entails. To such a person, it is consequently out of reach.

If I were to present you with a Grail, there would be no need for you to seek further. The Grail that you should all be seeking now is a new Grail—a world Grail.

And now I must leave you. May the light of truth shine upon you, now and forever more. *[a deep, resonant chuckle]* The human race must learn to laugh at itself. Laugh away those nightmares you have so industriously constructed around yourselves: a laugh a day helps you work, rest and play!

30 MERLIN, ARTHUR AND THE HOLY GRAIL

From the teachings of "Old Chinese", channelled by Marshall Lever.

It is known by the Guardians who are responsible for the physical plane that there is a need for consistent energy input into it. This energy can be put into it spiritually, and thus the Earth itself can maintain something of a balance. This energy always comes, causing a new creativity within your world.

But it is also known by the Guardians that, time and time again, energy has arrived in the world through physical beings who inspire, who create dreams, who allow those around them to imagine, who give others the beauty and the warmth of what could have been and what could yet be.

These energy cycles have actually occurred in periods of history. One you are concerned with is called Camelot. To create such an energy period or source, individuals of high evolution are chosen. They train in an etheric dimension close to your own, attuning themselves to conditions on Earth, understanding what needs to be done. They learn how to create vibration and to balance this or that reaction to it.

Such beings serve as the key, the energy, the nucleus, the generator, and are ultimately regarded as the soul of such a period.

Since the dawn of time, one specific group of creative intelligence have been materialising and dematerialising at moments of crisis. You know them as "Merlin". They have been called other things in other times. But they are a power source, a composite being identified as a single person who deals specifically with communication and keeping a dimension, or a "feeling", together.

As Camelot was to be an earthly training ground, Merlin again returned to your world, knowing what had to be done in the future. As the training continued, and Arthur and his companions returned to the spirit world, they began to see the signs of a very powerful energy, and a time when a unique situation would develop on Earth. A dimension that would converge on

137

the physical plane.

This energy-cycle, this dimension, was created then. And the reason that Camelot is so famous and looked upon now, is because so many of you, at one time or another, have longed to be part of a time when things were so exciting, when the teachings were so evolved, when there were quests and mysteries, when there was challenge and beauty. It holds its charisma because of the people within it, because of the warmth and beauty that they have, because of the power that they brought with them.

Merlin did not come through man and woman. He came through crystal. It is through crystal that all things are possible. It connects with every record, with everything that you have ever known, with everything you have ever been. It is the communicator and the positive traveller.

Merlin knew what he had to do. The people who converged he had to begin to pull together and thread together. He had to do this through one powerful figurehead—thus he sought Arthur. He found him and trained him. He taught him the ways of the forest. He taught him all that was a part of his knowledge, all that had been in other dimensions. Arthur began to struggle with it. He began to feel the difference. He was part of a new idea, of a new energy, with a guide or sage, with someone who had power beyond the physical world. And so he worked and developed, and tried to learn to make this dimension the dream dimension.

There is a need to dream. If you cannot dream of what has been and of the glory, beauty and strength of that time, you cannot dream of what you *will* be. For it is by dreaming that you transcend time, and it is through dreams that reality comes to you.

There was no recording, no records in those days, so a part of the role that Merlin played was to ensure that what was done there would be talked of for centuries; so that, throughout time, people would have something to look for, to feel, to aim for, to wish to be part of.

Merlin had the same energy force as did the Nazarene, centering back to the Essene order in the Middle East, and to

138

that of Dionysus and also the Pythian order in Greece. But the impulse or power goes beyond that: this was the manifestation of many spiritual energies coming into the world together.

The sages Lao-Tse, Confucius, Buddha, Zoroaster and Pythagoras were all aspects of the power behind Merlin—each of these masters embodying much the same energy, but bringing it forward and trying to usher in again a period that would be, for your world, a new light and a new life.

Finally, there are these things for you to consider:

You are all Arthur. Whether man or woman, you are Arthur.

Merlin is your higher self.

Excalibur is the hold you have on the present.

Misuse of emotion will cut you away from your higher self.

Camelot is what you create within your life, and the people you attract to it.

Morgan and Guinevere are the feminine element, the inner sanctuary, the garden, the beauty that is needed to balance the outer life.

Lancelot is the curriculum of your world, the conflict, the testing.

All these are symbols designed to give you a framework in which to gain experience in your own life.

You are in Camelot to dream, to search for the Holy Grail. Merlin holds it.

Find that higher self that is everything that you have ever been and everything you will ever be—that allows you to be all things, allows you to transfer and transmit into all worlds.

31 MISSION: EARTH

Many eventful years have passed since Merlin came into our lives in a small sunlit glade south of Glastonbury. During these years, friends and acquaintances have often asked us, "Who on Earth is Merlin?" and we have noticed that, each time, our answer is slightly different. Although we hope we are gradually coming to understand what he really is, and try not to limit him, we are always aware that words are quite inadequate to describe someone or something timeless, formless yet everpresent. One might as well try to nail down the wind.

And yet in his human guise Merlin is not the least portentous or forbidding. Impressive he most decidedly is, but he inspires affection rather than awe. He has an uproarious sense of humour which he frequently uses to deflate the futile, the pompous and the misguided aspects of human behaviour. He is no respecter of self-important persons, and does not suffer fools gladly. Offsetting this is his endearing gift of self-mockery.

As to his present purpose or mission here, it might be helpful to assemble some of the clues or pointers that have come our way:

Merlin has described himself as a member of "the Circle of Magicians". By which, we presume, he means a group of creative powers, dominions or archetypes. And so, "Who on Earth is Merlin?" isn't quite the right question after all! Yes, his influence *is* being felt here on Earth once again, but it is almost certain that he comes from another dimension or Universe altogether.

He embodies an ancient wisdom that easily transcends all the dogmas of religion and science. He does everything in his power to inspire in us a reverence for life on *all* levels, from the highest to the humblest. A master of space and time, he can and does appear in any guise he chooses, human or otherwise, physical or subtle. [When thinking about Merlin, I am often reminded of Wellesley Tudor Pole's comment about the Glastonbury Zodiac: *"So you see, we are here in touch with interstellar divinity."*]

Merlin consistently urges us to look within ourselves, to set our own house in order before we attempt to do the same for our community, our country and the world. He has on several occasions reminded us that only when we have managed to balance our inner and outer lives will we be functioning fully.

He is definitely *not* the being to dispense cosy celestial clichés and spiritual platitudes! His tactic is to stimulate, to challenge and to sting into action. He does not mince words.

He sometimes despairs at the sheer passivity of the human race which, for centuries, has allowed a few men in power to do all its thinking for it—and so hold us all in their thrall. "Think for *yourselves*!" he urges us, time and time again. And, in doing so, he is surely sounding the keynote for the next thousand years.

He never tires of reminding us of our privileges and responsibilities as custodians of the Earth and all its life forms—and of the appalling penalties facing us if we continue to abuse these privileges.

Ever since he re-entered our lives, Merlin has encouraged us to re-examine the Earth mysteries, numbers, proportions, harmonies, healing; and to investigate the hidden properties of light and sound. He seems to be steering us towards a study of the science of life itself. He cannot, will not, drop all the answers in our laps: he never lets us forget that we must do the work *ourselves*. He often nudges us in this or that direction, but leaves us to choose whether or not to pursue it.

As an archetype of creative intelligence, "M" first seemed to be part of a trinity of energies—the other two being what we have come to call "the King" and "the Lady", or Will and Love/Wisdom. Then a fourth, highly important energy made itself known—one which manifests in our urge for self-expression, laughter, spontaneity, music, dance, drama, ceremony, sport and merry-making. We presume that only by balancing these four prime elements within us can we become whole. [Merlin himself certainly does.]

"M" has lifted the veil and shown us brief, tantalising glimpses of the almost unimaginable future that is ours—if we can win the battle that is raging within each one of us. Above all, he seems to be encouraging us on our own individual quest. He is endlessly tolerant of our stupidity and self-importance, our self-indulgence and self-pity, our vanity and weakness of will.

He is always there when called, waiting with a joke or witticism—or a caustic aside that only partially veils the deep compassion and care with which he urges us along the path towards whatever it is we conceive to be the Grail—and ever onward to the ultimate reality that lies beyond even *that*...

One of the very first things Merlin said to me, back in 1975, was, "We have worked together many, many times, in many worlds." This alone, whatever it means—and I think you'll agree that such a statement, lobbed casually into the conversation like a grenade, has to be taken on absolute trust—was enough to throw an entirely new light on things. It certainly strengthened my resolve to keep right on to the end of the road, come what may.

We are now facing what is indisputably the greatest crisis in all our history. We live in a world of technological and other wonders—yes. But the crisis is here, standing like some eighty-foot tidal wave poised to smash everything in its path...

If ever we needed concrete evidence that there is, after all, a Plan for this world and this Universe—and that this Plan is being administered by wise and compassionate beings who have our welfare at heart, despite our reckless delinquency—it is right now. And that evidence is the reappearance during recent years of such guides, counsellors and friends as Merlin himself.

32 A BLUEPRINT FOR THE FUTURE

As the long, dark winter of the present Age at last gives way to the glimmer of a new spring, Merlin prompts us to project our minds into the approaching century.

No lover of woolly thinking or vague abstractions, he urges us to think in practical terms of the rebuilding of civilisation that must now follow.

What an awesome undertaking! And yet, "M" stresses, only when we realise how far we have sunk and how much we have lost; only when we find the courage and self-honesty to concede that our remarkable record of creativity and ingenuity throughout the centuries has been permanently tarnished by the catalogue of our crimes against each other, the planet and its many life forms, can that rebuilding begin in earnest.

How to go about it? First, says the Magician, by recognising our own personal flaws and imbalances, by forgiving ourselves for them, and by making a concerted effort to replace them with something more positive.

"Only when you have set your own house in order can you begin to help others to do likewise. That done, you can then turn your attention to your community, your country, and the Earth herself."

And let's not fool ourselves that it's going to be easy. Most of the systems that govern human society are hopelessly corrupt beneath the well-polished veneer of tradition and respectability. The history of virtually every institution we examine—political, religious, military, industrial, monetary—is riddled with the disease of "power and profit before people".

Our current educational systems have fallen disastrously short of their real purpose, as defined by the Universal Declaration of Human Rights.

There is enough for us *all* on this planet—and yet the poor and hungry number hundreds of millions. Still more millions live under the yoke of tyranny and oppression. We all live in the shadow of extinction: by tampering with the atom for illicit purposes, we have opened a Pandora's box of nightmares.

144

Institutions with vested interests have an infamous record of suppressing inventions and discoveries that could have benefited the human race enormously—because they felt that their power and profits were threatened by these discoveries. Persecution, ridicule, imprisonment and even murder have been the means of silencing the hapless inventors.

Madness! When the next generation of science and technology arrives, as it surely will—and I've got a hunch it won't be long in coming—there will be more than enough opportunity for the conglomerates and mega-corporations to convert to it—and make themselves even *bigger* fortunes! So what's the problem?!

Merlin promises us that, if we can outgrow this obsession with power and profit—"the bastard children of fear and greed" is how he once described them to me—a prospect of almost limitless wonders will unfold before our eyes. Wonders that will, once and for all time, evaporate the illusory man-made barriers that have long stood between science and so-called "magic", between the possible and the so-called "impossible".

Yes, even the Magician himself always insists that "magic" is nothing more than "using what is already here—for good or ill; to help people or to harm them."

Our leading physicists have recently been assembling a new model of the Universe and of ourselves—a model that not only enlarges our understanding of matter, but reveals the existence of forces and dimensions that can no longer be dismissed or derided.

Nowhere is this more neatly illustrated than by the recent discovery that the *outer* [cells, molecules, particles, atoms] are simply different manifestations of the *inner* [wave forms, impedances, interference patterns]. In other words, there *is* no such thing as matter after all—only a series of wavelengths or vibrations whose interaction has brought into being a vast range of *apparently* solid bodies.

Which is what the mystics have been trying to tell us all along!

These scientific advances, and the discoveries of open-minded explorers of ancient lore, have come not a moment too soon. Mankind seems in recent decades to have been undergoing a crisis of faith and identity. All our modern technology and scientific wizardry—all the King's horses and all the King's men, as it were—have not proved adequate to protect us from the approaching spectres of famine, disease and total war. Indeed, in many respects, scientists have contributed as much to the current crisis as they have to our well-being.

Perhaps the very word "science" is to blame for much of this: it means "knowledge", whereas scientists are explorers, forever reaching towards truth yet never bringing it entirely within their grasp.

Mystics, too, are explorers—of the mysteries. It would seem, then, that both scientists and mystics, so long entrenched in opposition, are in fact performing an almost identical function: investigating and attempting to codify, for our benefit, some of the laws and components of that ultimate mystery, life itself!

Today, computers and ancient lore are combining to place at our disposal the means whereby we can more easily understand our own nature and that of our host planet; the means to get the most out of ourselves and our surroundings—without the abuses and imbalances that have characterised our progress thus far.

Inevitably, much of our science, technology, industry, agriculture and medicine is about to be transformed by this alchemy. So it is hardly surprising that no word yet exists in our language to embrace the wide spectrum of new disciplines and methods that we must develop if, as Merlin has stated, the universal energies are to be tapped for positive and life-enhancing purposes.

The word we have been using, during our research in recent years, is now submitted for your approval or otherwise. It is:

> *holometry*—the art of demonstrating that since every part, or microcosm, contains and reflects the whole, or macrocosm, it is freely transferable and communicable to any and every other part of the

whole; a series of practical procedures proving this principle. [Greek *holos* whole + *-metry* suffix indicating instrumental procedures and systems]

Our awareness of matter, energy, space and time are all now undergoing quantum change. The revelation of this planetary moment—a moment of unprecedented crisis but equally great promise—is that we are about to discover the means to solve most of our problems, to expose the fraudulent systems that have held us all in their thrall for so long, and to free ourselves to pursue our rightful destiny.

If Merlin is right—and we have no reason whatsoever to doubt him:

"You are standing, quite literally, on the threshold of a cultural, scientific and human bonanza, the like of which has never been known.

"All of these things, and many more besides, lie within your grasp. But of one thing you may be sure—the key to this treasure-chest is the desire to serve your fellows and the world. The lust for power and profit will not open it.

"With all these marvels at your disposal, it is high time you drew up a blueprint for the future. It will require the goodwill, the resources and the commitment of every one of you who is dedicated to shaping the future. It will be a work of synthesis and networking, regardless of national, cultural, religious or racial differences. It will not be the work of governments—at least, not so long as they continue to embody the ossified attitudes and defective vision of the dying Age.

"This blueprint will almost certainly not be the work of one person alone—unless, of course, a contemporary Tom Paine is somewhere among you. If so, please make yourself known at once!

"For an age and more, you have been subsiding so far into matter that you have all but lost touch with the many subtle realms and intelligences that have never ceased to serve you. Yet even now, if you can humbly ask for their advice and co-operation, this blueprint for today and tomorrow, once drafted, can become a living, ever-evolving reality.

"Together we can begin to lay the foundations of a new world—the first human society *without* the seeds of its own destruction built into it.

"Who's for bringing the future a little closer?!"

"The timeless vessel of fusion is the Grail. As a vital symbol of receptivity, it has reappeared in the modern radio telescope, capturing subtle energies from distant galaxies. Within our hearts, the Chalice is our receptor for that mysterious force that binds atoms, plants, men, planets and stars together. That mysterious force is all around us—here and now—and the fusion is living in our music, our dance and our laughter."

Steve Hillage and *Peter Tuffnell*

33 TIME TO WAKE UP

One summer afternoon, as Pete, Bran and I sat in a clearing in Essex among the recently felled trees, Pete, on whom the burden of "bringing Merlin through" had fallen, challenged me to try.

It was early days in our renewed relationship with the Magician, and I was still rather in awe of him. But after all, I thought, I *had* first heard his voice in a wood, so what did I have to lose?

I shut my eyes, stilled my mind, and waited.

Almost at once I felt "the presence". It fell round me like a cloak, or the protective embrace of a huge pair of invisible wings.

And this I must record: from that moment on, whenever I asked, the voice came to me. It never failed. I didn't call it up every day; I didn't even invoke it often, because I still had the idea—maybe misguided, maybe not—that you shouldn't call on these exalted beings all the time.

Of course, if it isn't "them" at all, but some aspect of our own higher self that we invoke in this way, then probably we *should* feel free to call on it whenever we feel the need.

Anyway, the results of my first efforts in that clearing appear throughout this book, signed thus:

"M"

You might have found that they have the "right" feeling, and can therefore accept them. You might, on the other hand, now you know who channelled them, consider them quite inadequate. Fair enough. I must accept full responsibility for them, and I do. In which case, please bear with me—my "receiver" is not exactly state-of-the-art. By all means look around—or within—yourself for a more authoritative voice, one that *does* have all the hallmarks of the Magician.

And please, let me know what you come up with: I'll be the first to throw my hat in the air if it's the right stuff!

Because that, as it turns out, is what the quest is all about. Merlin has always emphasised that we can all be our *own*

150

teacher, magician, leader, call it what you will.

Inside us all, he reminds us, is a vast inner landscape containing deep reservoirs of knowledge, fathomless oceans of collective experience. And yet for centuries we have been programmed by successive powers-that-be to ignore the riches lying hidden within us, and to worship *outside* figures—messiahs, saints, saviours, kings, princes, emperors, dictators, politicians, generals, madmen, movie stars, pop stars, sportsmen, celebrities, soap stars, posers, publicity-junkies and the like.

Isn't it time we woke up?

Isn't it about time we grew up, put these fantasy parent figures and sex substitutes aside and started to give *ourselves* a little respect, to credit *ourselves* with talent and ideas and intelligence?

Why *should* anyone else expect our slavish adoration?

Why *should* we live our lives through someone else's?

Why *should* anyone tell you and me what to do, what to believe and whom to worship?

Surely you and I have the right to shop around and form our *own* conclusions about the obstacle race/roller-coaster ride/magical mystery tour called Life!

"The long, dark night of empires, isolated nations, blind obedience to leaders, religious dogma, suppression of entire peoples and marching honourably to death beneath bloodstained banners is passing. An age of exploration, discovery, synthesis, sharing and self-determination is dawning. Awake! Awaken others if you can."

"M"

34 DEAR FRIEND, TAKE HEART

A message we received in 1986 from one of the Masters of wisdom who serve humanity—and have always served us—unseen and largely unacknowledged:

At last your race has begun the long journey back towards the light. Out of your current struggle will arise the perfect vehicle for showing how the love of the Creator can be made manifest on the physical plane.

That vehicle will be the heightened consciousness that even now is spreading among you, a consciousness which recognises that there is a better principle than self-interest for organising human civilisation, a more sublime philosophy than materialism upon which to build your future.

It is tempting to lose hope amid the terrible reports of famine, war and death. It is easy to withdraw into apathy before the awful spectre of nuclear devastation. Yet if you refuse to take action, you literally condone the treachery of the ones who even now are plotting to lay waste the Earth garden.

But what *is* the most effective action to take? There are Beings on many levels who are working incessantly to rescue this beautiful planet from destruction at the hands of humanity. Whether you conceive of these Beings as angels, space brothers, guides or guardians makes little difference: they are here and they care deeply about the plight of the Earth.

But they can make their influence felt only through those who are in physical bodies—yourselves. They *must* have your co-operation if they are to contribute to the healing and transformation of the Earth.

There are many ways to serve in the great programme of rescue that has been initiated. Some seek forcibly to oppose the authorities whom they see as misguided or evil. They protest, demonstrate, and thus prick the conscience of their less dedicated brothers and sisters. They serve according to their perceptions.

Others promote change through the political process, believing that good government will encourage a corresponding goodness in the citizenry; that moral rectitude can be imposed from above. They too serve according to their perceptions.

Yet there is another way for those of you who would promote peace and sanity in the world. And that is literally to become channels of light, through which the Beings we have mentioned can transmit into the Earth plane their own special vibrations.

By gathering together in groups of like-minded companions, you can make a vast difference to the balance of light and darkness on this planet. By joining in prayer for peace and protection, or by meditating together, by visualisation, invocation or concerted action, you can call down a ray of divine power to calm the storm.

We urge you again to lend your energies to the great project of rescue.

Upon *your* dedication rests the fate of the world.

Hilarion.

35 LAST CHANCE

If we think of the Earth as a body—the seas as its lymph system and the nations as organs—then we can see how disastrous and unnatural war and international hostilities really are. Espionage is a kind of leukemia, war a malignant cancer.

What if our liver declared war on our lungs? Our larynx on our kidneys? Ridiculous, you say. Impossible. Yet this insanity has been allowed to go on throughout history! What the body of the Earth desperately needs now is a brain and a heart. And since no one nation qualifies for either role, the brain will have to be a repository of every kind of useful information, the sum of our collective knowledge—to which every nation contributes and which is freely available to all.

It is the withholding of this information that has caused all the blood-clots in the world's arteries.

A heart?

It has always been here, but has never been able to function fully—the collective yearning of every human being who deplores war and poverty, injustice and the rape of the planet, and says, "Surely there must be some *other* way!"; the collective concern of everyone who recognises that we are all one, and can no longer ride roughshod over our mother, Earth.

It is high time the governments of the world had the courage—and honesty—to hold international referenda on such topics as armaments, nuclear technology, the distribution of wealth, and war. And to abide by the resulting majority vote in each case. After all, governments are meant to reflect the will of their peoples, and not the reverse.

There can be little doubt which way 99% of us would vote if we were presented with the following choices. Correction—not *if*—we *are* being faced with these choices, right now:

PAIN	PLEASURE
DISEASE	GOOD HEALTH

DOGMA	CHOICE
FAMINE	PLENTY
DECAY	GROWTH
DESTRUCTION	CREATION
PREJUDICE	OPEN-MINDEDNESS
POVERTY	WEALTH
VIOLENCE	LAWFUL ACTION
PORNOGRAPHY	LOVING
THIEVING	GIVING
VANDALISM	CREATIVITY
DICTATORSHIP	GUIDANCE
UNEMPLOYMENT	FULFILLMENT
IGNORANCE	INFORMATION
ISOLATION	CO-OPERATION
EXPLOITATION	EDUCATION
DEGRADATION	SELF-RESPECT
DESPAIR	HOPE
FEAR	JOY
RACISM	TOLERANCE

Presumably our vote goes to the right hand column above. But remember, none of these desirable states will be dropped in our laps. Indeed, people and institutions with vested interests will do everything in their power to stop us achieving them.

I don't have to remind you that the press and television news every day are devoted almost exclusively to the *left* hand column. It's as if we're being *programmed* with negativity, conditioned to believe that this is a perfectly normal state of affairs—and that it will always be.

Well a whole lot of people dotted around this benighted planet know otherwise—and are already doing something about it. We are rapidly approaching critical mass—the moment when the concerted force of reason and logic and love and compassion will outweigh that of darkness and destructivity—and *then* just you watch the seesaw go bang!

"Look to your children. Do you not see it in their eyes?! They *know...*"

"M"

"It's up to you! Yes, you!"

John Lennon: *Instant Karma*

36 EXIT THE WIZARD

Even though we have enjoyed a special relationship with "M" for several years, it took quite a while to discard the traditional image that most people have of him—that of the crotchety old sorcerer of myth and legend.

But remember what happens to Dorothy and her companions in the Emerald City at the end of their quest? The Wizard of Oz reveals that their notion of him is an illusion, and that what they have all been searching for so desperately lies within *themselves*...

We have come to know more about what Merlin *isn't* than what he really is:

He isn't a person at all, in our understanding of the word.

He doesn't go about in a cloak and pointed hat, weaving spells and performing conjuring tricks.

He isn't of this world.

He doesn't even come from the Great Bear constellation—though we believe he does use it as a way-station of some kind.

He isn't an angel or extraterrestrial as such.

He is one of the constituent energies of this and every other Universe: creative intelligence.

He can appear whenever, wherever and in whatever guise he chooses.

What's more, he is *part of every one of us*.

An aspect of our higher self, which we can all call on when the going gets tough or we need some vital information.

He is the sage who enjoys being consulted. The Magician who exults in the sheer joy of creation.

He is an aspect of God the Father.

The Lady is an aspect of God the Mother.

The King and the Master of Ceremonies are their kin, maybe their offspring.

Together they build Universes, seed galaxies, oversee systems. They reach effortlessly through space, time and dimensions to touch you and me. All *we* have to do is turn on our receivers.

Limitless, benign energies. Imperishable, infinite.

The ultimate proof of our own exalted status, our divine origins.

Like the man said: *"Who could ask for anything more?!*

MICHAEL DEAN

37 THE PATH TO THE GRAIL

One summer afternoon, having assembled the first draft of this book, I decided to take a few hours off. At tea-time I called into St James's church in Piccadilly, where Petey and his merry band were running *The Whole Bookshop*. There I met John and Caitlin Matthews, and John kindly gave me a copy of the book he had just put together: *At the Table of the Grail.*

Towards the end of this work was a chapter by Dolores Ashcroft-Nowicki, *The Path to the Grail,* the most lucid and inspiring description of the Quest that you could hope to find. It explained so much of my life and that of my closest companions that I immediately showed it to them. They were all deeply moved, and encouraged.

I felt that I had to write to the author, thanking her for clarifying what has so long been shrouded in mystery and secrecy, and for demonstrating just how relevant the Quest is now, despite—or possibly because of—the pressures of modern life and the sophistication of today's science and technology.

Judge for yourself. Maybe you'll find here echoes of your own life:

The Quest of the Grail, like all things in this cosmos, has a grand design that must be followed: a pattern, a sequence of steps in the great Dance, steps that are ignored at one's peril. In the mystery schools this pattern is followed exactly and the student actually becomes the hero or seeker, and undergoes in his training an interior journey that follows the ancient design.

By such means he condenses many lifetimes' experience into one, and absorbs the understanding that such experiences bring into a shorter span of time. But success depends on his ability to follow the pattern, make the right choice of path when a crossroads is reached, and above all to ask the right questions at the right time.

In this the serious student is helped by a tutor, a kind of personal Merlin, who has already taken this road, and who has returned; the return is the most important part of the whole

Quest. It must be fully understood that the seeker enters upon the Quest not only for himself but for his race, and indeed for all those who cannot go for themselves, those for whom the time is not yet right.

The journey undertaken by the seeker is a paradoxical one: on the one hand, it draws the mind inward to the heart's centre, the Hall of the Table Round where sit the many facets of the personalities used by the seeker down the ages.

On the other hand, it also projects the mind outward, seeking to bring back to the everyday world an understanding of what has been experienced within. Seeking also to share that experience as far as it is possible with those who stayed behind.

He who seeks, finds, and returns, becomes a Janus-like figure standing at the gateway of many possible worlds. His eyes are unlike those of any other man. They see more deeply, shine with more wisdom, and weep more bitterly. Such a one is forever set apart from those he serves, and it is by his own choice. To serve well, one must first learn to stand alone and apart, and to observe quietly.

The Quest has three stages:

> 1. Separation from all that is known and loved. In myth and fairy tale this stage is enacted when the young hero or heroine leaves home and family, usually an aged parent who grieves most bitterly. In real life it is the moment when the soul hears the inner call and realises its need to seek out its sources, to renew itself in the Grail of Grails.

> 2. The journey, the danger, the wonder, the transmutation of the soul through experience. It is a time of training and study during which the student will be severely tested in real life.

162

3. The all-important return, bearing within the heart's centre, the gift. This gift is a transmuted Table Round, now made concave and fashioned into a personal Grail. It is filled with the essence of love, understanding and wisdom distilled from the knowledge donated by all those personality facets, the distillation of myriad lifetimes.

Such a Grail is borne with only one purpose: to let all *who can* drink from it. But the bearer of such a Grail can never drink from his own vessel, he must seek another who will give him to drink from their heart's cup.

The wine from such a chalice can be both bitter and sweet; we can never know until the moment of tasting. The true initiate is one who tastes both with equal joy.

The Grail may still be sought and won. Each man may be an Arthur, wise, loving, but knowing his own weakness. He may be a Lancelot, brave and strong, but easily led. At the end of the Quest he will be a Galahad, embodying all the good with less and less of the bad.

Every woman may be a Guinevere, royal but wayward, enchanting but heartless, but she too will come to the Chapel Perilous as Elaine the Grail Maiden.

We all go through a form of Quest in our everyday lives, but it is only when we reach a point in those lives when it becomes essential to seek, to dare, to know, and in knowing to keep silence, that we enter consciously upon the inner journey.

Whatever name the quest goes by, it is nothing more nor less than a return to that Source whence we came, and where we may find renewal.

"Take heart: you are *not* outcasts on a small planet, drifting aimlessly in Space. The Earth is only one starship in an immense fleet that is turning the corner and sailing to glory…"

"M"

38 THE NEVER-ENDING STORY

"What I am attempting to do now is to catch something, however, faint, of the flavor and fragrance of the Grail itself. The Christian faith has no monopoly of this mystery. It is not only 'older than the rocks,' or older than all the land and all the sea across which it moves and over which it hovers: it is older than the minds of men, older than the beauty of women, older than the worship of the gods, older than the orbits of the stars."

John Cowper Powys

In her monograph Guarding Merlin's Enclosure, *Debbie Rice reveals the direct relevance of the Arthurian legend to all our lives:*

One of the most composite and enduring symbols carried deep within man, especially within the heart of Britain, is the most holy Grail, and the Round Table. Like the Ark of the Covenant, the Grail has several meanings. It doesn't matter whether it can be historically *proved* that Merlin, King Arthur, the Knights and Ladies or the Round Table itself ever existed in physical form. What they *symbolise* is everything. And what they tell us is as relevant today as it was then: here is nothing less than a blueprint or guidebook for life on Earth—for every man, woman and child. Each one of us, whatever our background or circumstances, is to be found among the cast of characters in the Arthurian saga. And not only our role, but the *purpose* of our lives.

All we need do is ask, "Which character am *I* in this story?!"

KING ARTHUR
The competent earthly ruler. Man standing at

165

the brink of wisdom and enlightenment. His nobility is that of character rather than of parentage.

MERLIN
The Archmage. A great archetypal symbol of the man who, by deduction, has successfully extended his perception beyond the consciousness of the five senses and mere reason. He served and guided Arthur in the affairs of his kingdom, teaching the young man to work with the soul senses guided by intuition.

The four hero Knights:
PERCIVAL
The youth, suspecting that earthly existence is not all, sets out to explore the primeval forest, seeking the court of the King. But it is not the Grail court at which he arrives, but the court of Arthur, seat of worldly talent, efficiency and enterprise.

GAWAIN
Somewhat more mature than Percival, Gawain already has a place at Arthur's court. He senses a wider quest and sets out on his journey— even though he only dimly perceives its true purpose and goal.

LANCELOT
Possessing both the wisdom of his King and the intuitions of his Knights, Lancelot is more individualised than the other three hero Knights, but finds himself still tied by his love of worldly things—hence his fatal attraction to Guinevere.

GALAHAD

Galahad personifies the full realisation of human potential. The offspring of Lancelot and Percival's sister, Elaine, he arrives at the bridges and is admitted to the holy lands.

Other Knights of the Round Table include:

BEDEVERE
The friend you would trust with your innermost thoughts and secrets. A companion for all seasons, in times of peace or war.

HECTOR
Stalwart, trustworthy, balanced, earthy; lacking in vision he may be—but in battle, Hector is the man you would most want to see fighting by your side.

The Ladies:

VIVIEN
The Lady of the lake. Merlin's feminine counterpart, keeper of the sword Excalibur.

GUINEVERE
Tender, good-hearted, unprepared for the sacrifices her rank demands of her, she is torn by conflicting loyalties.

MORGAN
Companion and loyal friend of Merlin, working in secret to protect Arthur and his kingdom from their sworn enemies.

ELAINE
The Grail maiden. Loving and forgiving, she is the purest expression of feminine energy.

But as we know, duality, or opposition, is the governing principal of this world: day/night, good/evil, rich/poor, win/lose, illness/health, strength/weakness—these and many other pairs of opposites provide the arenas in which we can act out the drama of our lives. And so, we not only meet "the good guys" but "the bad guys" too. The interaction between them has fuelled almost all our history, literature, drama and cinema. In the Arthurian saga, the chief "heavies" are:

MORDRED
Said to be the illegitimate son of Arthur himself—or, according to other versions, the vengeful, demonic son of Morgause and her husband, Lot. Arthur's sworn enemy, and the instrument of his undoing. The King was doubtless aware of the danger Mordred represented, but probably didn't believe that any man would stoop to such vindictive schemes.

MORGAUSE
Ruthless and ambitious, she uses her beauty and power without scruple, in order to achieve her ends.

The Hallows of the Grail:

THE CUP
The vessel of essential stillness, *standing within us all*, silent, motionless and forever blessed. Its base is the bottom of our spine, its stem our spinal canal. The bowl commences at heart level, rising to the throat and ending at our head.

THE LANCE
The instrument that connects the inner and outer worlds: its shaft extends from the base of the spine and rises up the spinal cord, carrying

all communications from outer to inner worlds. It descends through the motor processes of our body, returning the messages from the inner to the outer world. Thus the two halves of the circular shaft are constructed. At heart level they widen into a diamond-shaped head, passing up through the throat and end with the tip of the blade at the pituitary gland. The lancehead hangs over the centre of the Cup, so that power can flow into it.

THE SWORD
The sword has many connotations, most of them masculine, but primarily it denotes the will of the spirit, and is therefore neither masculine nor feminine, but a synthesis of both. It must be wielded with knowledge and skill, and should only be used as a means of clearance and protection.

THE SCABBARD, or DISH or STONE
The earthly experiences—and the formulation of character—from which we draw the Sword.

THE NAILS
These equate to our emotional, mental and spiritual make-up. The site of operation is the hands and feet. They enable us to be in the world yet not of it.

THE CROWN
The Crown of thorns relates to the head: the back of the head is the doorway to other dimensions, permitting freedom of travel and expression between spirit, soul and body. The golden Circlet in Grail stories is only worn after the dragon—our lower self—has been mastered.

The relationship between these hallows and those of the Christ story are self-evident. In fact, they pre-date both Christian *and* Arthurian sagas by several millennia, and are living evidence of "the golden thread" of Ancient Wisdom that originated in Atlantean times or even earlier, and has somehow survived to this very day.

The roles played by the four hero Knights deserve closer examination:

PERCIVAL

The name Percival gives us a distinct clue as to the nature of his role or function: *percé* = pierced, *voile* = veil. He sees through the veil separating inner and outer worlds. [In scientific terms, this simply means he recognises that the physical plane is only part of the entire electromagnetic spectrum.] His duty was to undergo the ten initiations or degrees of human perfection:

the awakening:
he sets out on his quest

baptism:
he receives his Knighthood

temptation:
his first adventures

transfiguration:
he sees beyond the physical

illuminated living:
the quest for the Grail

crucifixion:
he encounters strong opposition

descent into hell:

170

he visits the land laid waste and comes to the graveyard perilous

resurrection:
he is united with his mother and sister

service in the kingdom:
the battle with Red Chaos and events within the Castle Mortal

ascension:
Percival, his mother and sister enter the chapel of the sacred Hallows

GAWAIN

His experiences are associated with expansion of consciousness which is accomplished in several stages:

learning discretion and discrimination:
he faces the Dweller at the Threshold—the embodiment of his own lower self and all his past misdoings

rebuilding the foundation:
by leaving the ruins of old, outdated beliefs, habits, ties and interests

reversal of focus and direction of consciousness

rectifying or replacing outworn symbols, patterns and structures

the victory of self-liberation

the evaluation of the triangle of body, soul and spirit

offering of the Sword:
surrender to the higher will

the vision of the Grail:
a glimpse of the Ultimate

LANCELOT

His course was to travel through the astrological signs, to experience the value of each principle illustrated, and to apply that principle in daily life. His twelve assignments were:

reasoning mind
[Aries] : the house of self-recognition

material mind
[Taurus] : the house of possessions and possessiveness

constructive mind
[Gemini] : the house of ideas and imagination

contained mind
[Cancer] : the house of self-consuming flames

the dawn of spiritual mind
[Leo] : the house of the ideal

intuitive mind
[Virgo] : the house of growing awareness

balanced mind
[Libra] : the house of partnership of heaven and Earth

initiate mind
[Scorpio] : the house of personal rebirth

the illumined mind
[Sagittarius] : the house of leadership

universal mind

[Capricorn] : the house of wisdom

elder brother mind
[Aquarius] : now appointed regent of Arthur, Lancelot is made "Champion and Protector"

Christ mind
[Pisces] : house of surrender—having been tested, Lancelot is freed at last from his earthbound prison

GALAHAD

As the conception of Galahad took place on the inner planes, the child could not reach full consciousness through his parents, so he was taken to a holy place. From the beginning, Galahad had contact with higher kingdoms. His instructors were twelve in number, indicating that, like his father, he had to learn life lessons epitomised by each of the twelve principles of the Zodiac; then he had to learn to take his place in the court of Earth.

At the Grail Table, each Knight sat on a chair bearing his own name and title, his rightful place on Earth. At that Table one seat is vacant—the siege perilous. So holy is this seat that if unworthily occupied, it engulfs the sitter and casts him into limbo. Each of us must seek the empty seat within ourselves, and achieve the degree of perfection that permits us to occupy it.

Galahad's victories lead him to progressive degrees of attainment:

the shield of the blood-red cross:
allegiance to a higher will

the red seven:
battle with the seven deadly sins—when the battle is won, seven red roses are placed on the cross

the white rose:
conflict with others less advanced, who include those
nearest and dearest to him—at the centre of the seven red
roses is placed one white rose

the seven pink roses:
final tests and initiations—a white rose is now placed at
the centre of seven pink roses

the blending of the roses:
now Galahad is within the community, assisting mankind
in civilisation's progress: the seven roses merge into one
great rose, with eight outer petals of white

the rose triumphant:
the vision of the Grail, covered in white samite: the white
rose comes to full flower in a universal dimension, with
star rays of the perfected soul radiating from its heart

And so the four hero Knights each found his place:

PERCIVAL
established new horizons by means of his water journeys
—representing *emotional* insights

GAWAIN
the man of air, accomplished the hard mountain-climb of
intelligence

LANCELOT
through *action*, brought emotion and intellect into balance on Earth

GALAHAD
gathered them all up in the form of creative fire

But there is always this to remember: none of these roles
is preordained: at any time, if we so desire—or if we receive

174

powerful impulses from our inner selves that more could be learnt or achieved by doing so—we can break the mould and take on one of the other roles available. How many times have we heard of someone who rejected the role for which life had typecast him, and went on to greater things?

The reverse is true, of course: at any moment, by ill-choice, or as a result of some other negative impulse, or repeated self-indulgence, we can destroy everything we have built up, and bring ourselves to ruin and disgrace.

We are the captains of our own Fate, the masters of our own soul. There *are* no deities or powers arbitrarily deciding what we should be or become. It is this fact above all that we should bear firmly in mind as the coming century—and the coming Age—draw near.

Because if we do, the horrors and tragedies of the past will never be repeated.

39 ACROSS THE HORIZON IN OVERDRIVE

It was midnight exactly as I finished reading one or two passages from this book to my good friend James Bell, a generous and unfailingly receptive audience—the kind all writers thrive on!

We discussed the crisis facing science as it reaches territory that is going to turn most of our dogma, scientific *and* religious, on its head.

I then said I felt there was one last thing this book needed—a message, afterword or parting gift [although he isn't leaving, of course] from the Magician himself. A capstone to round it off.

"Why don't we fasten our seatbelts," said James with a grin, "and ask Merlin to take us across the horizon in overdrive."

There was an immediate knock on the pine chest beside my desk. We both recognised it and laughed.

"The Magician is In," I chuckled, reaching for a pen and paper.

I went into receive mode. Moments later I felt my breathing slow, then deepen. I could sense "M" coming closer, and cleared my throat.

At last he spoke: "How often am I asked, 'Merlin, tell us this, tell us that.'" A deep, thunderous sigh, slowly fading to silence.

"You press me to reveal what you already know, if only you would take the trouble to look within. The world needs no more teachings, no more tenets, no more theologies and belief systems. And especially, no more dogma.

" 'All you need is here,' if I may paraphrase John Winston Lennon, a budding initiate whose achievement many of you have recognised.

"If I were asked to condense all I have to say into a single word, that word would, in all probability, be:

SHARE."

A long silence followed. I began to wonder if the Magician had withdrawn. But I could sense he knew that we would welcome anything more he had to say. Always more...

Suddenly he resumed:

"As you approach the foot of the holy mountain, its peak still veiled in cloud, you are sensing that the game is up, that your obsession with matter is an illusion, and that you are about to undergo a head-on collision with ultimate reality.

"When the breakthrough comes—and it is only moments away, on the hands of the cosmic clock—all the man-made laws and mechanisms that have held you in their thrall these many centuries—the politics of confrontation, secrecy, espionage, dogma, the military machine, social hierarchies and the like—will no longer apply, because that breakthrough, by its very nature, will reveal such mechanisms to be irrelevant.

"It will finally be proved that *you* belong to the planet, and *not* the planet to you; that the human race is a single organism on the surface of the biosphere; that all energies, terrestrial and cosmic alike, are free, having been placed at your disposal for a purpose, and can no longer be hoarded, withheld and charged at so much per unit!

"When you wake from your long and troubled sleep, you will see that there *is* a Plan for humankind.

"These discoveries will trigger an explosion of creativity such as the world has never seen. Technology will never be the same again. Do you know what the word means? This might come as something of a shock to you—it means 'the science of industrial *arts*' and comes from the Greek word *tekhne*, meaning 'art'! And what has it become?! It has become the watchword of blinkered materialists and technocrats immersed in lifeless, soulless permutations of a once-inspired field of discovery.

"When the veil is lifted and the mountain-top revealed, it will be as if a vast treasure-chest has been flung open and all its wonders are being poured over your heads.

"Never forget, these treasures are not external, bestowed on you from on high, but aspects of *yourselves*, released at last from the wellsprings of your being.

"This great moment will signal the beginning of yet

177

another chapter in the drama. You will rediscover your real identity, your inner powers, and the purpose of your tenancy of this lovely world.

" 'For instance?' I hear you say. 'Come on, Merlin, give us a for instance!'

"All right, you shall have one. No, you shall have more than one:

"You will discover what the atom really is.

"You will learn who *you* really are.

"You will harness light, and you will decipher the secrets of sound.

"You will diagnose and heal as if by magic.

"You will light and heat and power your outer lives—virtually without cost.

"You will communicate not only with each other, but with beings from other worlds, other dimensions.

"You will release the creator in yourselves.

" 'Ordinary' people will daily perform what you now call 'miracles'.

"All this will unleash a tidal wave of joy and relief, goodwill and fellowship that will sweep away much of your pain, your suffering and your guilt.

"And when that happens, listen hard, my friends... and you will hear the whole creation singing, *'Halleluyah! They are coming home!'* "

40

11 August, 1987

Dear Ava,

Thanks so much for phoning—and for sending that high-octane chocolate cake! Strangely enough, despite your news,* your voice has never sounded better. Whatever you might think, I've a strong intuition that what you have been through this year is not the end of the story at all, but a major personal hurdle you had to clear before the next chapter can begin; and that during this new phase you'll be working on more cylinders than ever.

The garnet is a little gift. It has been charged at one of England's most potent energy centres, so if you ever feel a bit low, hold it in your left hand close your eyes for a moment and feel the light building up around you. The powers of gemstones are something we're beginning to look into, and an excellent book someone sent over from Washington says of the garnet:

"It corresponds to physical circulation, the energy principle, and the haemoglobin factor in the human body. It is a co-operator with mankind, helping to energise and restore the circulation, and assist the kundalini into its proper pathway up the spinal column…"

And to think that for centuries we've used gems just for decoration!

The sparkly notebook is for you to write down your innermost thoughts, or whatever. I know you've sworn never to write your memoirs, but I reckon that, rather than endure a whole string of scissors-and-paste jobs by people who have never even met you, you're the only person to write about the extraordinary inner and outer journey that has been your life.

* [a stroke, affecting her vocal chords]

Louise Brooks, Hildegard Kneff and Shirley MacLaine all wrote brilliant memoirs, and you're in a unique position to tell us about the golden days of Hollywood, so-called. By talking into tapes, if you don't relish the prospect of filling up reams of empty exercise books!**

And now back to the future: I believe you have a key role to play in the awakening of human consciousness that is taking place today and will continue to accelerate until this century ends. Your presence, your voice and your power can make a very considerable contribution in days to come.

You must have noticed how people's search for truth, and protest against everything that is repressive and demeaning, are intensifying. The lies we've been told for centuries are being exposed, one by one. Groups are forming throughout the western world to bring in alternative ways of thinking and of dealing with age-old problems.

What has all this got to do with you? Everything! You are known for your honesty, your frankness, your contempt for everything that's phony. For years, without knowing it, you were embodying the spirit of today.

Scientists, journalists, doctors, teachers, actors, writers, "ordinary" men and women, even politicians—the wave is building up at terrific speed. And in years to come, it is going to transform the media, communications, education, transportation, industry, agriculture—you name it. Meanwhile, you're already doing far more than you think, just by being yourself.

Enough! I'll call round soon, if I may, and retrieve the two screenplays—both of them now under radical revision. I'll keep you posted on MR UNIVERSE. Knowing me and where I'm at, you've doubtless sussed that MR UNIVERSE is not about bodybuilding, but something else altogether!

Love and admiration from Michael.

Throughout our long, mysterious and indescribable friendship—Ava and I were utterly unalike, lived in different worlds, yet shared moments of quite extraordinary, almost mystical intimacy, as if our souls knew each other far better than our physical selves, and shared secrets no one else would even understand—I used to think it was no accident that she was so admired by the likes of Ernest Hemingway [she made three pictures based on his stories] and John Steinbeck.

Both men recognised in her a kindred spirit, a free soul who had no time for pretence or pretension, was nobody's fool, worked, drank and played hard, swore even harder, was true to her own very personal code, wouldn't hear a word spoken against those she loved, rode with the punches, and could neither be bought, packaged, corralled nor controlled. In order words, a good trouper.

It is also worth noting that whereas Ava played Guinevere in the otherwise none-too-distinguished movie *Knights Of The Round Table* [1954], Steinbeck himself, haunted by the Arthurian legends throughout his adult life, was inspired—obsessed almost—by the notion of chivalry and honour, which he felt had never entirely died out, and were virtually man's only chance of redemption; closely identified with Lancelot, came from America to live and work in Somerset on two occasions, determined to translate Malory's *Morte d'Arthur* into modern English, and soaked up the atmosphere of Glastonbury and the West Country on what was clearly his own Grail quest.

**[Which is what she finally did: a total of ninety tapes that became AVA (Bantam Books), her own account of her remarkable life and career—a document as uninhibited, truthful, funny and brave as the lady herself...]

181

41 THE CEREMONY

One night in 1987, I had a remarkable dream. Pete came to see me, unannounced.

"Quick!" he said. "We've got to hurry, they're already preparing."

My apartment vanished, and we found ourselves in a vast hall with no ceiling. The Guardians were all present, and countless other beings whom I didn't know were packed in on all sides.

Standing in the centre of them, facing the King, was a young man whose face I couldn't see. The King placed a sword horizontally on the man's outstretched hands.

> THE KING
> You are the one. Wield this wisely.

The young man nodded, but said nothing. And then the Sword itself spoke:

> EXCALIBUR
> The fire in your heart called me up from the waters of Life. Feel my cold steel, old friend. I am the ultimate weapon you have so often dreamed of, sought, invoked: the Sword of the Angel of Light.
>
> By your charge, I serve all who are about to serve the world. I am the Sword of Truth and Life, *not* of death and destruction. So sharpen my blade, then cut the ties that bind mankind.

The King stepped back, and Merlin took his place. He took a simple gold circlet and held it above the man's head.

> MERLIN
> Wear this well, my son. Know who has worn it

182

before you. Serve the world as they did. Respect all life. Forgive, as you would be forgiven. Uphold truth, honour and justice. Let compassion be your armour, and humility your shield.

The key to all this is the children. These children who are not children have come to take their planet back.

This is a battle such as the world has never known. And remember: you will have *two* armies fighting with you, not just the one.

Merlin lowered the circlet onto the young man's head. Although he still didn't speak, I picked up the man's thoughts clearly: he was incredulous, overwhelmed that he of all people had been snatched out of obscurity to receive these honours. I kept trying to figure out who he was. And then the penny dropped: It was Man himself. Everyman. Mankind. *All* of us...!

The Magician stepped back, and the Lady appeared. She held a glowing crystal chalice over the man's head. Her expression was filled with such love and compassion that it would melt even the hardest heart. It was just as well that the man's eyes were lowered, I thought. At last she spoke:

THE LADY
The emblem of the passing Age has been the Cross—symbol of mankind suspended in time and space. The emblem of the coming age is the Grail itself. A new Grail, a world Grail.

Humanity is waking at last from its long and troubled sleep; darkness is giving way to the dawning of self-knowledge, self-respect and self-reliance.

Your task is to see that the coming battle is not

fought in anger, nor in a spirit of revenge. How could it be? The enemy is *within*, not without! Arm your soldiers with the most powerful weapons of all—love, logic and laughter.

There will be victories, setbacks, delays and still more victories. But keep your mind and heart clearly focused on what is at stake—and you'll win this Battle before it has even begun.

May you walk in the light of truth and love, wisdom and joy, now and for ever more.

The Lady withdrew, and there was a moment of absolute silence that seemed to vibrate with faint, subliminal music. Though he was armed with the sword of Truth, and was now wearing the crown of Justice, the man clearly felt naked and insignificant amid such company—and woefully unfit for the task that lay before him.

Merlin made an almost imperceptible gesture in his direction. This seemed to bring the young man out of his reverie.

With great solemnity, and suddenly remembering what was expected of him, he bowed deeply, once in each of the four directions.

First, to the Lady.

Then to Merlin.

To the King. And finally to the Buddha, who had noiselessly taken his place to the east, and was sitting in the lotus position, smiling his now scrutable smile.

7. FULL CIRCLE

42 A BOLT FROM BEYOND

The following extracts from my diary highlight a particularly painful yet memorable transition from 1989 to 1990:

Mid-December, 1989:

> ELLEN phones, says, "Watch the last week in January—it'll all start happening—it'll be time of major change, corresponding with the new *cyclic* time, which is to replace the *spiral* time we've been living in..."

New Year's Eve:

> I do some stock-taking on my word-processor—make up a list of the people who have been important to me in my life. Included is a tribute to AVA, and a comment about the inner rather than outer nature of our relationship.

Tuesday night, 23 January 1990:

> While TONY and I are working, I go into the kitchen to make yet another cup of tea, and hear myself say, "It'll be a miracle if they can keep AVA here long enough to work with us..." For once TONY makes no comment—he has always been 100 percent confident of the inevitability of AVA's role in our future...

Wednesday night, 24/25 January:

> I have a dream: my sister AUDREY appears, saying she has been in the presence of this fabulous LADY who was "holding a reception for these stars—and they all had jewels in their hair".

"Maybe they weren't diamonds so much as emblems of their spiritual rank," I reply.

I won't realise the significance of this dream for another twenty-four hours...

Thursday, 25 January:

Throughout the morning a terrible wind scours the British Isles... I consult ELLEN in Oxford, and she says it is a kind of planetary spring cleaning in preparation for the arrival of the new energy: a fine balance of feminine and masculine—with more emphasis on compassion, tolerance and co-operation than we have known before.

4 p.m.

ELLEN calls, says she has just heard on Radio 2 that AVA has died of pneumonia. I call TONY, JAMES, MERRYN and AUDREY. I'm devastated—and stay that way until TONY arrives in the evening...

10 p.m.

He says, "Come on—look what happened to your life when ALMA died! *[The veil lifted, revealing a new Universe altogether.]* Well it'll be the same now AVA's gone—she'll really start to kick ass for us now...!"

I immediately feel better. I remind TONY of my dream about AUDREY—and we realise it was a direct warning of what was about to happen. Despite myself, I laugh.

"I can just imagine AVA arriving upstairs at that reception, looking around and saying, 'Where the fuck is this?!' and to the LADY, 'And who the hell are you?!' and the LADY replying, 'I'll tell you later, honey. Now you go off and enjoy yourself—there's a whole lot of friends waiting to see you...'"

Monday, 29 January:

The British press have given AVA an incredible farewell: almost full pages in every paper, and in some, double-page spreads. Nearly every headline contains the word "Goddess".

Yeah, I'll buy that: if the LADY decided that, soon after cinema had been invented, two representatives of herself would appear on the screen in quick succession—two perfectly complementary incarnations of her own power and beauty: one of them mysterious, inscrutable and alluring, the other earthy, voluptuous and untamed—who better than GARBO and GARDNER?!

January 31:

Back-up arrives for ELLEN's explanation of that wind a week ago:

I call AVA's secretary BETTY KEAN, and she says, "It was uncanny, Michael—just before AVA died, at 10.15 in the morning, it all went absolutely quiet and still—the balcony windows were open, and outside in the gardens not a leaf stirred. Then she died. And at that very moment, the gale started..."

188

MICHAEL DEAN

Let AVA have the last word:

A BOLT FROM BEYOND

GOD spake when Ava Gardner died last week
—the Hollywood legend had telephoned her
old friend Peter Evans a few days before, to ask
him round to her Knightsbridge flat, but the
best-selling author of biographies of Aristotle
Onassis, Bardot and Peter Sellers, pleaded that
he was too busy finishing a novel.

"She was always calling, sometimes at three in
the morning, but this time she told me she was
going to die and would I come over and write
her obituary? Naturally I did not want to
believe her and she ended the conversation
with the words, 'When I go, it won't be quietly—I'll send you a bolt of lightning.' "

Sure enough, Evans duly heard from Ava from
the other side: a massive branch of an oak tree
in his Dulwich garden smashed through the
roof of his Californian-style house, missing
him by six inches as he worked on his word
processor.

"A third of the house was destroyed," says
Evans. "In the absence of Ava, who wanted me
to write her biography, I'll have to contact my
insurers."

Mail Diary, DAILY MAIL, 31 January 1990

43 FULL CIRCLE

On the morning of the July 1991 G7 Summit in London, James and I packed my books into his car and set off for Evesham, in Worcestershire. I had been asked by a prisoner there if I could help him create a library for the inmates and had agreed to lend them my own.

As the car turned into the Marylebone Road, a hundred yards or so from my home, James decided we needed some music to speed us on our way. He selected a tape and was inserting it when his hand accidentally turned the radio on for a split-second—just long enough for us to hear a woman say, "Oh, Ava!"

We burst out laughing. I looked up at the sky through the windscreen and said, "Hi, Ava! How's it going, honey? What's happening?"

At that moment a traffic cop materialised in front of us and held up his hand.

We stopped.

And across our path rode two motorcycle outriders, a black armoured stretch limo containing President Bush, another pair of outriders, then a second stretch limo containing President Gorbachev. Two crowded Secret Service vans brought up the rear.

"I don't believe this!" said James, as the traffic cop waved us on and we headed for the overpass. "Do you realise just how much orchestration that took—first Ava, then the two Presidents passing only a couple of yards away from us?!"

But that's only the half of it:

When we returned to London early in the evening—the books having safely reached their new home—I switched on the BBC 9 o'clock news.

The entire bulletin was devoted to the historic agreements reached by the two Presidents at the Summit, earlier in the day.

I was listening to the last ten pages of my screenplay Catch The Lightning, *almost word for word!*

A screenplay that virtually every television network in the

UK and America had turned down flat—most of them saying, "Do you *really* imagine that the Soviet and American Presidents would attend a Summit hosted by a British Prime Minister in England, agree to reduce their nuclear stockpiles and usher in a period of real co-operation and exchange of resources?! Come on, sweetheart! How naive can you be?!"

And here, seventeen years after I first drafted it, the whole darn thing had come true—right down to that motorcade, those speeches, and the written protocols that followed them...

One last piece of the jigsaw, for your amusement:

Ava had agreed to play the US President's wife, Gayle Forman, a former actress—and a lady with a mind of her own. ["Gayle Forman", you won't be surprised to hear, is an anagram of "Morgan le Fay". Sorry, but old habits die hard!]

There's one scene in particular that Ava would have eaten alive:

As her husband is unwell, she brings some lunch on a tray into the Oval Office, where he is conferring with his special envoy, Neill Halliday, and the Secretary of State, Herman Kleindorff.

While she is setting out the food on a table at the far end of the room, the door opens and General McCorquodale, a Pentagon warlord, marches briskly into the room. He doesn't see her.

THE PRESIDENT
General.

McCORQUODALE
Mr President. Herman.
[ignoring HALLIDAY, he indicates
the Satellite PHOTOS on the desk]
The Soviet Union is almost certainly
preparing to go east for her grain.

THE PRESIDENT
And you suggest?

He indicates a chair, but McCORQUODALE prefers to stand.

> McCORQUODALE
> What we should have done years ago,
> before this phony honeymoon began:
> an immediate pre-emptive strike -
> land, sea and air.

> THE PRESIDENT
> Forget it. The United States will never
> deliver the first blow. Not while I'm President.

> McCORQUODALE
> Don't you realise there won't *be* any second
> blow in this shooting match!

> GAYLE FORMAN [VO]
> Now you listen to me, Mister...

> ANOTHER ANGLE, WIDER: All eyes are on the First Lady.

> GAYLE FORMAN [contd]
> Have you ever heard yourself on playback,
> General? You're totally obsessed. There's
> only one thing on your mind...

McCORQUODALE is staring at her in disbelief. KLEINDORFF darts a quick glance at the PRESIDENT, but the Chief Executive's expression is unreadable.

> GAYLE FORMAN [contd]
> Have you ever thought about the *shape* of guns
> and rockets and bombs and missiles, General?
> They're not based on any part of the *female* anatomy,
> that's for sure!

> [the growl of a bitch leopard]
> They're an extension of violent, aggressive,

frightened little boys.

Tell me, why are you so hooked on size and power?
I'll tell you. You're terrified the next man might have
a bigger one, or know how to use it better. Terrified
a woman might laugh at you and kick you out of bed.

A choking sound comes from the back of McCORQUODALE's throat. MRS FORMAN holds up a hand to forestall any protest.

GAYLE FORMAN [contd]
I know, I know, ladies in White Houses
aren't supposed to throw stones. But
God dammit, General—enough is enough!

She goes to the door. Turns.

GAYLE FORMAN [contd]
You don't represent the will of the American people,
Mister. Nor do *any* of the world's military strategists
who believe the answer to every problem is to frighten
or blackmail everyone into submission—or blow them
away.

You've drugged us all with threats and fear and
secrecy until we hardly know what's going on any more.
But people are beginning to wake up. And when they
do, your kind, thank Christ, will be out of a job!

She stalks out. A short, electrified silence follows. GENERAL McCORQUODALE is boiling with rage and humiliation. HALLIDAY is trying desperately not to burst out laughing.

At last the PRESIDENT breaks the spell:

THE PRESIDENT
You know, General, I get the distinct impression
that we've just had our wrist slapped.

And you know what I reckon? That as Ava stalked out of the Oval Office, having delivered that little missile of her own, viewers would have cheered...

MICHAEL DEAN

44 THE WIND OF CHANGE

With the impeccable timing that has long since ceased to surprise me—I have now come to accept such startling synchronicities as normal—a publisher friend has just sent me a truly remarkable book to edit, *The Wind of Change*. It is by far the most detailed, specific, encouraging—and sometimes astonishing—portrait of our immediate future that I have come across since reading the prophetic work of Vera Stanley Alder some years ago.

It was channelled by Julie Soskin, who was recently contacted by a cosmic intelligence that clearly wished to impart some vital information. When Julie asked who or what was the source of the incoming material, the reply she received was, "a synthesis of energies of higher consciousness—Original Thought."

Does that sound familiar? It reminds me of Merlin's own description of the "Circle of Magicians" to which he belongs: "We are notes in a cosmic octave. But each note is itself a multitude of octaves of different frequencies, and when we sing together, the Universe resounds to our song."

This impression was redoubled when I found in *The Wind of Change* such echoes of Merlin as, "Nothing is lost" and, "Nothing is wasted". Categorical statements of this kind, I suspect, can only be made by detached yet compassionate beings who *know* that Creation never squanders its resources and that Nature herself always recycles her energies.

Here, then, are a few appetisers from this book of treasures:

So far you have lived to a large degree by the laws of cause and effect. But we tell you now with certainty that this will come to an end...

There will be a balancing of energy and then the energy will turn to light. There will be no darkness on your globe. Even the days will be affected. Your sun is changing, and in a short space of time there will be another source of light...

Every individual has an energy. That energy is what you call the soul. Your souls are energy. The soul functions something like a battery within you. A soul that is clear and unlocked permits greater brain facility, provides a strengthening of the spiritual body and the pure love beyond emotion. Within three to five years at the most, there will be scientific proof of the energy that you call your soul...

Harmony will then be felt with other individuals and a kind of group consciousness such as you have never experienced on this planet will come into existence. There will be no more striving and straining to be better than the next person. There will be a kind of love without emotion, but so pure that each individual will know what any other individual requires at any given time...

For many, many years you have longed for a society in which people truly care for each other. Now you are coming to a time when members of society will truly care and know what the needs of others are, and therefore such things as famine and poverty will not exist. *This* is your perfect society...

There is a link between peoples of the Universe and very soon there will be, in your words, interplanetary movement. It enables you to free yourself from the burden of the physical—meaning in reality the spirit inside yourselves goes where it chooses and takes the body with it. This will provide such a freedom of spirit as you have never known and cannot even now comprehend. All we can say is that you will be and are gods...

Men have cherished ideals of united countries, a united world: Utopia. They have tried to achieve it through the inadequate means of governments and policies and politics. It never worked then because of the temptation of the ego, but we tell you that soon you really will have your perfect community...

You will have no need of government: there will truly be government by the people. There will be unity. We can tell you clearly that there will be no leaders. All will lead and all will serve...

Children go to school now to learn to read, to write, and they will still learn those things then. Writing will still be needed, but there are many other things that children learn now at school which will no longer be necessary, and so they will eventually not be taught...

Children will be taught by their parents, by those around them and by the school of life. Remember that your children will be more evolved and stronger than you are today, and everyone will live longer...

Eventually there will be no need for electrical communication of any kind. Why pick up an external instrument when you have a superior one within you by which to communicate with others? There will be no need for mechanical vehicles either. Why climb into a cumbersome vehicle when you can be anywhere you want in a moment without it? And there will be no need for metal birds in the sky because *you will all be able to fly*. You may think this is just poetic imagination on our part, but we tell you that it is real...

Those of you who expand in light will notice how fit you become. You will have no illness or disease, and if needed your bodies will repair themselves...

There will be a new perception for sight. This enhanced

sight will gradually bring about a change whereby the individual will be able to see inside things physically: the veins of trees, the skeletons, the bones...

The accelerated energy is affecting the hearing too. Human hearing is beginning to receive frequencies and sounds much higher than its usual pitch. People are beginning to hear everything. They can even hear the sound of leaves growing on the trees...

Do not be afraid or fear the changes; they are dramatic, but when things become redundant they will disappear as a natural course of events...

After the period when the individual has awakened and blossomed like a flower, the predominating power and energy will be very different from before. Your body will need time to get used to it and will very likely be the last thing to adjust, but once there is a synchronising of the energies of mind, body and spirit, you will have strength and power beyond your wildest dreams...

Eventually, all will be able to channel their own information. This is not a select, elitist procedure - it is open to all...

The heightening of energies is allowing you to take an enormous step in evolution, because you will be comparable to and like the angels. Imagine for moment the difference in energy between what you are now and what early man, the cave man was. We do not exaggerate when we tell you that it is an even greater step you are now coming to. This will open out for you a totally new perception of life and the ability to soar to greater heights on all levels of existence...

We want you to break down all the defences, barriers and structures you have built up—not for destruction's sake,

198

but because on breaking down those barriers you will be able to see further, you will be able to see *everywhere*…

Your gods *must* be dissolved. THERE ARE NO NEW GODS. It is time to acknowledge and fully realise at last that you yourselves are God…

We see you at this moment as beacons of light, golden light, shining brightly all around you. Know that this is what you are and you will be healers of *the world*…

We do not exaggerate. That is what is happening. It is to a large extent because of a natural progression, a natural development, and it is also because of the winds blowing. You will see for yourselves this new reality —a new perception that will be dazzling to you…

You are nearly there.

45 DREAM

I wake up on a settee in an unfamiliar, darkened room. A young woman with black, shoulder-length hair is sitting on the floor. She leans forward and hugs me—it's too dark to see her face—then suddenly she is gone.

Three black women come in and tell me I'm wanted in the recording studio. I accept this without question, even though, despite my deep love of music, I'm neither a musician nor technician.

I go outside. The house is surrounded by low brick walls and, beyond them, rolling hills. Everywhere there are kids. I have brief conversations with some of them. They are relaxed and worldly, oozing self-confidence and positive energy.

Away in the distance I see a pastel, elliptic-topped building. The ground is soft and bouncy as I make my way towards it. Each side of the building is a different colour; the nearest is blue.

I enter through glass swing doors and walk along a series of pale blue corridors, then go into a small sound mixing room. I sit down at the console. In front of me, behind a plate glass window, three girls are playing extraordinary music. I can't see them so much as feel their presence, and I feel quite comfortable with that.

When they finish I go into the studio and discuss with them everything I've just heard. There is a whole new style, sound and instrumentation here; now they play me music by kids of many nationalities—Russian, Chinese, Hungarian, Argentinian, Greek...

Young, modern, energising, it all seems to be speaking the same language. Shit, the musical barriers are coming down!

I hear accordion on feedback, trumpets used as percussion, xylophones with wow-wow pedals. And those voices! How do they *do* that?!

I leave the studio and, as I make my way back through the pale blue corridors, they seem to be rising like an elevator. I carry on walking, and still I'm going higher until the corridors

200

dissolve and I find myself floating in a bubble, in what could be mist or cloud.

Gradually an opening appears in the mist. In front of me are twelve fully-armoured Knights, some sitting or reclining, others standing, two on horseback. The horses are protected by the most intricate armour I have ever seen. My focus on all of them is razor-sharp—every hair, every rivet, every link of chain-mail is piercing in detail. Their eyes are so alive; the colours are metallic blue, black and white.

It is not in my nature to speak in public, and I am never comfortable with formal ceremony, but at this moment I feel it right to hold out my arms, raise my voice and deliver a speech to the assembled Knights with total power and authority.

Don't ask me what I said—I can't remember, except that it must surely have been about what is coming—but they all looked towards me and seemed to understand what I was saying.

When I have finished, a white light envelops everything and slowly I begin to descend, until I am back in the blue corridors and walking towards the glass doors where I came in.

Sitting at a table on bench seats by these doors are the three girls from the studio. I sit down opposite two of them, the third is on my left. Now they are visible.

They are in their early twenties and beautiful, casually dressed in a contemporary, individual style. They are drinking milk-shakes and talking to me. The girl opposite slides a bowl of orange ice-cream towards me and gives me a spoonful to try. It is fantastic, unlike anything I've ever tasted. The ultimate food.

As I am oohing and ahhing and they are laughing, the girl next to me puts her arm round my shoulder and hugs me. I look slowly around at the face, the black hair, the eyes...

It is AVA.

Tony
Hollywood, 1991

I, too, dreamed of AVA, late in 1991: I found myself in her London apartment. People were coming and going. AVA was about twenty-four, devastatingly beautiful in a very laid-back sort of way, her short hair curly at the ends and glistening, as if she had just been swimming.

She saw me—"Hi, honey!"—took my hand and led me outside. As we walked uphill, arm in arm—in some kind of moorland, not the Knightsbridge gardens I had expected—she smiled suddenly, as if something amusing had just occurred to her.

"So we *do* get to make a picture together, after all! The biggest movie ever made, with an international cast—and cost—of *billions*. The story of the end of one world and the birth of another. A story that reaches back into legend and history—and forward into an absolutely mind-blowing future.

"The saga of a race of people waking from a long, agonising nightmare and fighting their way back into the light. And of all the unseen friends who are arriving to help them.

"Yes, *our* story. A real-life adventure involving every single one of us. An epic struggle that's gonna end in triumph—and you better believe it. But in this production, there are no featured players or extras—we're all *starring*! *And* co-directing."

She laughed that irresistible AVA laugh, her head thrown back.

"How about *them* apples?!"

202

MICHAEL DEAN

Surrey, 29 September 1991

Dear Michael,

Thank you so much for your book. It arrived on Friday and I set about reading it straight away. Oh, Michael!! So many puzzles solved, questions answered, confirmation of my own inner journeys, and at last a name to put to the wonderful creative energy I have felt coaxing, leading, pushing and gently guiding me onwards for the past few months.

I have constantly asked, "Why me?" feeling inadequate to the enormous task I feel is on the horizon, but The Return of Merlin *has helped such a lot: now that I know I am only one of a vast army of souls being led towards the same goal, I can go on with more confidence. Recently, everything seems to have speeded up, with so much knowledge, so many things and people coming into my life all at once. All the tests and trials of the past years are apparently bearing fruit, and at last the pieces are coming together, just as you say.*

By Christmas I hope to be in south west Scotland where I feel my real work is to begin. I needed your book at this time, to put more pieces into place and to confirm that I have not been sidetracked into a blind alley.

The Egyptian connection you picked up with me was accurate: I have a strong link with Thoth, who first led me onto the right path and still helps to guide me to the the knowledge I need. I must have had a good Egyptian incarnation at some time, because he has helped me all my life and brought me into the vibrations of energies and beings that both help and need me. It was Thoth who led me to the Great Hall where I met the energy that has helped me over the last few months—[Merlin?].

Yes, I'm sure from your descriptions of, and messages from, him it's the same energy.

Thank you so much. Love and light, Eileen Palmer.

London, 1 October 1991

Dear Eileen,

Thank you so much for your letter—written on Michaelmas day! Now, perhaps, you know why I was driven [yes, driven!] by "M" to produce a private edition of this book and to send it to whoever was attracted to it. It is, I suppose, a gift from him to some of the good folk who are soldiering away in the front lines at this crucial moment: far more copies have gone out to people I have never met than to my own friends.

How right you are to speak of "the enormous task I feel is on the horizon" and "a vast army of souls being led towards the same goal"— especially your choice of the word "army"! I think we can be sure that Merlin and the Lady—and the Archangel Michael and his battalions—will be guiding and inspiring this army, too!

It is as if, day by day, the screenplay BATTLE FOR THE EARTH is coming to life in the real world around us. But this one won't be the whirlwind of destruction and death on a global scale that has so often been prophesied, but a huge cleansing and rebuilding operation. And when it's finally over, surely there'll be the biggest celebration the world has ever known.

You aren't alone in being guided to the right material at the right time: I was sent THE WIND OF CHANGE just as I was preparing and revising this book. What a revelation! It not only confirms everything Merlin predicts about our near future, it goes into considerable detail about that future, and so provides the perfect "afterword" to my own book—a capstone to round the whole thing off. How brilliantly—and unfailingly—our "friends in high places" orchestrate and arrange our affairs!

I wish you every success in your mission in Scotland. You ask, "Why me?" and you are the answer to that question: your humility and dedication are the badges of your rank as a commissioned officer in the Battle to come! Everyone will serve, according to their talents and perceptions, in days to come. There won't be any "other ranks", as they are so ungallantly termed at present—we are all *being commissioned this time…*

Oh yes—your letter gave me great encouragement too; so you see, it's a two-way thing, with no debts or obligations on either side.

Thank you!

Onward! Upward!

Michael.

46 MAKING MAGIC

Have you ever thought how curious it is that, slap bang in the middle of our sophisticated technological age, with all its micro-miniaturisation, computers, Space missions and other marvels, the practice of magic should persist? Throughout history, pharoahs, emperors, monarchs and heads of State are known to have employed sorcerers and sooth-sayers. Yet even today, Governments still engage the services of mediums and occultists when it suits them—though don't expect them to admit it! Such dramatic headlines as, *"Police raid farmhouse—seize heroin with street value of £3 million!"* are just as likely to indicate the use of psychometry and dowsing as of more conventional methods of detection. I have already mentioned that Winston Churchill himself was advised by an initiate of high degree throughout World War II—and thank God he was, because, as is now widely acknowledged, Hitler was the instrument of some very sinister characters indeed who, had they not been thwarted, would cheerfully have sacrificed even *more* millions of their fellow human beings on the altar of their grandiose schemes.

In case you yourself have ever wondered about such things, I asked Peter Quiller to let me have his thoughts on practical magic in our own day, and am most grateful to him for the following—which arrived the very next morning!

The questions I am most frequently asked during my travels are, "How can *I* become a magician?" "Are there any spells or rituals or incantations I should perform?" "Do I need any special clothing or equipment?" And I confess that I invariably reply with a couple of questions of my own:

The first is, "What *is* magic?"

And the second, "Why do you *want* to be a magician?"

You might be surprised if you knew how few of my questioners have even asked *themselves* those two questions!

I believe Michael has already quoted the definition of "magic" that Merlin himself gave us, almost twenty years ago:

"Magic is the practice of achieving certain effects or attaining certain goals by using *whatever is already available*—nothing more and nothing less. Whether we use it to harm others or to help them is, of course, a matter for our own conscience—or common sense!"

In other words, magic is far more likely to involve the intelligent use of existing materials than the summoning of supernatural powers. I grant you, certain very rare—and highly trained—persons have been known to invoke supernatural agencies, for good or ill. But that doesn't concern us here. I have known people who can conjure a three-course meal out of a virtually empty food-cupboard. *That* is real magic. Glenn Hoddle's and "Magic" Johnson's long-distance passing—*that* is pure magic. The ability to win a smile from a child who is angry or upset—that too is true magic.

But if—despite all cautions and warnings—you insist on studying magic, do please bear in mind "M"'s old adage, "The twin of power is responsibility." The careless or malicious use of the energies can only rebound on the user; just as the constructive use of them can only redound to his credit. So now for a few rituals—or ceremonies, as I prefer to call them—which I trust you will find helpful.

THE CRYSTAL INVOCATION

In order to approach the four Guardian energies, it is necessary to obtain four different types of crystal and arrange them on the ground at the four points of the compass.

First determine where in the night sky the four constellations associated with the Guardians are located at the time of your invocation [a planisphere will help you to do this].

The four constellations you require are:

Ursa Major, the "Big Bear"—the Magician
Cassiopeia—the Lady
Draco, the Dragon—the King
Orion, the Hunter—the Master of Ceremonies

Now place the appropriate stone at the nearest cardinal point to each constellation—preferably in advance of where the constellation is in the sky. The following crystals are often used as "agents" of the four energies:

The Magician—amethyst
The Lady—rose quartz
The King—citrine
The Mystic [or Master of Ceremonies]—jade

Once you have created your "circle of power" [I suggest you make it of manageable dimensions—a 31-footer might be a bit "over the top"!]—kneel or sit on your heels facing North. Once you feel yourself beginning to fill with energy, bow three times to the North [forehead touching the earth each time].

Move your receptive hand into the centre of the circle, palm downwards. [I presume you already know which of your hands is essentially the "receiver", and which the "transmitter".] You will be directed to one of the four crystals. This is the energy that will now communicate with you. [The aspirant does not command the energies: the energies direct the aspirant!]

Now move round the circle to the position of the Guardian who has accepted you; place his or her crystal against your forehead, look skyward and ask your question. Keep your eyes closed and concentrate on your question. The answer will usually be given in a "mind picture" or visionary experience, either immediately or within 24 hours. If it is not, the problem night well be within yourself!

You may ask any of the Guardians to make their presence felt in your life for some constructive purpose: to help you develop as a person, maybe; to grant you clear sight or perspective; to re-align your physical energies; to enhance your health and well-being; or to assist you in a difficult task. If you try to command the Guardians, or invoke them to harm others, the energies will rebound on you. Anything negative you wish on others must harm *you*.

FIND YOUR GUARDIAN

Astrologically, the four Guardians are associated with the following constellations:

The Magician—Leo/Virgo
The Lady—Aquarius/Pisces
The King—Scorpio/Sagittarius
The Mystic, or Master of Ceremonies—Taurus/Gemini

The four signs not included above are mixtures of the two Guardian energies they "balance". Such people tend to be more centred in their ways, more amenable to other points of view. Capricorn, Aries, Cancer and Libra are called the "cardinal" signs and are often deemed the "strongest" in the Zodiac; whereas the "fixed" signs of Taurus, Leo, Scorpio and Aquarius are regarded as stable or sustaining. However, the "mutable" signs of Gemini, Virgo, Sagittarius and Pisces are seen as the most elusive and unstable.

From this we can deduce that the Guardian signs are combinations of opposites. People born under the various Sun signs mentioned above are automatically subject to one of the four Guardian energies that permeate the cosmos; others are heir to *two*! For example:

CAPRICORN is under the aegis of the King and the Lady.
ARIES is under the aegis of the Lady and the Mystic.
CANCER is under the aegis of the Mystic and the Mage.
LIBRA is under the aegis of the Mage and the King.

When consulting a horoscope it is advisable to look at *both* the signs connected with one's appropriate Guardian. "Cardinal" types, however, can look at the signs on either side of their own Sun sign for indications of Guardian influence.

ATTUNING TO THE LOCAL LANDSCAPE

There are three basic telluric energy currents, and they operate in straight lines, gentle curves, and spirals. In order to understand your locality, it is necessary to find and identify these three energies around you in your home and garden—if you are fortunate enough to have a garden, that is!

Consider carefully your favourite spot in the house or garden—the place where you instinctively feel most "at home" or relaxed. This is obviously infused with the kind of earth energy that suits you best. [As you have probably noticed, cats and dogs are excellent indicators of energy spots.]

Use a pendulum to determine which energy pattern the site exhibits. [The pendulum may describe the energy path, or a series of "Yes"/"No" responses.] Having found your own personal harmonic shape, proceed to locate *all* the places around the house where this specific energy exists. You may find that you have to move your bed to a more congenial spot because of this!

You will probably find that you cannot stay in your favourite haunt forever, because the energy shifts or "changes". Some days you will find you are in a "spiral" mood; on others, you might feel "straight"; and at weekends, you might favour gentle curves! The energies constantly alter, as do we ourselves from hour to hour and day to day: what suits us one day will be uncongenial the next. When we are able to "read" our own energy shifts, and those of our surroundings, we can begin to commune with our local landscape in a way that was never possible before. And remember—even earth energies can be "off colour", as we are from time to time when something upsets our system.

MAKING A MAGICIAN'S WAND

Select a type of wood you feel most comfortable with—oak, ash, beech, for example—or perhaps something rare and unusual to which you are drawn. Make your wand according to ancient Sumerian dimensions: 19.8 inches, 39.6 inches or 79.2 inches long, depending on your intention—and maybe on your own physical stature!

The wand should be bound by three bands of metal, evenly spaced—gold at the top, silver round the middle, and copper at the base. You must be quite sure what you intend before fashioning a stave based on these ancient measurements. The construction should take place in a spirit of deep contemplation. Once finished, the instrument will take on a life of its own and will collect and transmit energy continuously. In order to "switch it off", you should wrap it in black cloth—preferably silk—and keep it with such crystals as amethyst. Never underestimate—or abuse—the power of this device, or it could be your undoing!

THE CANDLE INVOCATION

If you wish to "far-see" something or someone at any time, you can do the following—preferably outdoors:

Create a "circle of power" with crystals aligned to the cardinal points of the compass. Place a single green candle in the centre of the circle, with a small dish of salt on one side of it and a chalice of pure water on the other. Depending on the position of the constellations at the time, the salt and water should be placed to favour the Lady/Mystic [water] and the King/Magician [salt].

Kneel within the circle, facing North—traditionally the place of darkness and mystical knowledge—and concentrate on the person or place you wish to far-see. Light the candle and gaze into its flame for at least thirty minutes. Then close your eyes and let the images come to you. You should now be able to see the person or place in question.

It is important to keep a stilled mind during the whole meditation. If you experience difficulties, you can adapt the crystal invocation [above] and ask one of the Guardian energies to help you locate the object of your attentions. They may or may not comply, but it it is worth a try. On no account use this or any other ceremony to spy on others or intrude on their privacy. Such activities come within the compass of "dark" or dubious magic, and you would only be creating a rod for your own back.

VISITING AN ANCIENT SITE

Before you visit any ancient site, first attune to your own local landscape and become familiar with earth energies and their funny ways. And be sure that your own energies are in harmony before setting out on your expedition. Prepare for about a week before the event; adopt healthy routines and take special care with your diet. Plan your route carefully; follow old pilgrim paths if you can, and travel wherever possible on foot. Approach the site with due reverence and *ask permission* to enter! Then and only then should you enter the sacred precincts.

Your first task is to find *your* place within the site. Walk around until you sense the kind of vibration with which you feel most comfortable. Be assured that there is such a spot at every site, even though it might move from day to day.

Having found it, still your mind and let the site *talk* to you. Have no preconceptions; just let the energies of the past— or even the future!—flow through you and over you and absorb whatever you can. Note everything you see or feel or experience at the time; you might be amazed by what the site can tell you!

You will know when it is time to leave, and you must do so at once. Make your farewells, and say a special "Thank you" to the individual "watcher" who guards the site. Then depart without a backward glance. When you are a good distance away, you may then make another farewell. If you fail to observe these few rules, you will most likely lose everything you have learned: you will simply not be able to remember anything. Believe me, you will *know* when an ancient site has taken you into its confidence!

So there it is. I hope these few ceremonies and observations will help you graduate from aspirant to apprentice to magician. And remember, your own motives and intentions will colour everything you do. It was ever thus, and—I suspect—ever will be!

Michael Dean

47 STATE OF THE NATION

"What has *happened* here?!" a dismayed American friend asked me in the departure lounge at Heathrow airport last week, moments before he flew back to New York after a short holiday in England. "Someone or something has sure beaten the bejesus out of you people."

I could hardly disagree: all too clearly, we in Britain are experiencing not only the bitter aftertaste of a decade of reckless, smash-and-grab economics, but also the malignant cancer of the current political process [half the country dragging its heels because "*they* are in power, and screwing it all up"]. As if this were not enough, we are having to endure the rapid decay of our education system, widespread unemployment, the continual erosion of standards of honour and decency, tolerance and civility; not to mention a perceptible loss of nerve, sinking morale, spiritual bankruptcy and general apathy!

Recent royal scandals and misadventures have revealed two things: first, that only when protected by distance from their subjects can kings and queens maintain their semi-divinity; and second, that many of us still require a focus for our national pride—a receptacle for the deep, almost mystical affection we have for our homeland. In their own time, King Arthur, Queen Elizabeth I, Shakespeare, Christopher Wren, Raleigh, Nelson, Yeats, O'Casey, Walter Scott, Robert the Bruce, Dylan Thomas, Lloyd George and Churchill all personified some aspect of the genius of their nation. The Queen fulfils a similar, if formalised, function today.

But in years to come, who will be chief custodian and standard-bearer of the spirit of these islands? Irrespective of the future of the House of Windsor—and of our new role as members of the European Economic Community—there now seems to be an urgent need for a physical symbol of our national pride and identity.

This could be provided by a new building of spectacular beauty and setting, funded by public subscription and containing the Hallows of Great Britain—Crown jewels, Magna Carta, regimental flags and battle honours, first folios, treasures, works of art, models of great inventions; and an archive containing documents and objects of national interest and importance, particularly those related to the future, as our future is no less important than our past. These hallows could be chosen either by a Council of Elders or by public debate and referendum. And a written Constitution of Great Britain—which is, in any case, long overdue—would set a seal on all of them.

Although neither palace nor museum, temple nor cathedral, concert hall nor gallery, assembly chamber nor exhibition centre, the proposed building could embody elements of all the aforegoing. It would be open to the public, and ample seating would enable visitors to absorb the spirit and atmosphere of the place and all it contains.

If the term "United" Kingdom is ever to lose its ironic and somewhat reproachful flavour, we will have to learn to live without our ancient hatreds and prejudices. Meanwhile, a national shrine in the honoured tradition of Tara or Camelot—one that transcends all differences of race, creed and culture, while reminding us of the incomparable legacy we share—might serve to bring that eventual goal a little closer. By means of television, we could all be present at the consecration ceremony.

48 THE HOPI PROPHECY

Elsewhere in this book you will have come across Merlin's exhilarating vision of our future—a future which, bearing in mind the daily diet of tragedy, violence, pain and death we keep inflicting on each other, might seem too good to be true.

The mystery of the perpetual struggle between our higher and lower selves—angel wrestling monster, Jekyll versus Hyde, good guy versus bad guy, call it what you will—has been one of our major preoccupations throughout the Ages. A most intriguing explanation of this ongoing saga has only recently come to light, and I am deeply grateful to Peter Fuller, in whose extraordinary book *RISING OUT OF CHAOS—The New Heaven and the New Earth*—a dramatic personal view of the return of the Light to a planet shrouded in darkness—I came upon the following:

THE HOPI—the people of Peace—OUR LAST HOPE

The Hopi are directly descended through the Anasazi from the Mayans, and are part of a migration of native peoples from the south with totally different genetic roots from the majority of nomadic, carnivorous plains Indians—Apache, Navajo, Sioux etc.—who migrated from the north. The Hopi have always been a peaceful, domestic race, operating by consensus rather than force, and husbanding the Earth in deep attunement to the grains and vegetables on which until recently they lived. Surrounded first by predatory northern tribes and then by meddlesome and subversive whites, the lot of the "people of peace" has not been an easy one.

Throughout their ordeals, however, certain of their elders have retained the spiritual knowledge and prophecies of their Mayan forebears, especially those that refer to what they call "the transition from the 4th to the 5th Worlds" in the days leading to their "Omega point" of the year 2013.

This period is known as the time of the "Rebirthing of the World" and, according to their teachings, humanity must pass through nine "Worlds" before achieving completion. Their prophecies warn those aware enough to recognise and act upon them of negative thought patterns, and certain critical events to look out for at this stage of our evolution. Since they have been so liberally—and often inaccurately—interpreted, I feel it might be helpful to summarise here their particular relevance to us all.

THE ESSENCE OF THE HOPI PROPHECY:

THE BALANCE OF LIFE

As caretakers of life, we affect the balance of Nature to such a degree that our actions determine whether the great cycles of Nature bring prosperity or disaster. Thus our present world is the unfoldment of a pattern *we* have set in motion, and our divergence from the natural balance is traced to a point preceding the emergence of the physical form we manifest today.

Once we were able to appear and disappear at will, but through our own arrogance, we took our powers as instruments of Creation for granted and neglected the plan of the Creator. As a consequence, we became confined to our left and right sides—the left side (right-brain hemisphere) being wise, and the right (left-brain hemisphere) being clever and powerful—but unwise and forgetful of our original purpose here.

THE CYCLE OF WORLDS

This suicidal split was to determine the entire course of our history, for Age after Age. As life resources diminished, in keeping with the cycles of Nature, we would try to better our situation by means of our own ingenuity, believing that any mistakes could be corrected by further inventions. Through sheer cleverness, most people would lose sight of humanity's original purpose and become committed to a world of their own design, which would ultimately oppose the order of the Universe itself. Such people would eventually become the mindless enemy of the few who still held the key to survival.

In several previous worlds, the majority advanced their

technology in this way even beyond what we know today, and the consequent violations against Nature and fellow humans caused severe imbalances that were resolved in the form of war, social disintegration and natural catastrophe. As each World or Age reached the brink of annihilation, there remained a small minority who managed to live in nearly complete accord with the infinite Plan, as implied in the name, Hopi. Towards the final stages even they would encounter signs of disintegration within, as well as receiving enticing offers and severe threats in the outer world aimed at forcing them to join the majority.

OUR PRESENT WORLD

Our common ancestors were among the small group who miraculously emerged from the previous world as it underwent its destruction, although they too were tainted with corruption. The seeds of the crisis we face today were brought with us when we first set foot on this planet. Upon reaching our present world, the Hopi set out on a long migration to meet the Creator in the person of Maasaw, the caretaker of this land and all the life-forms upon it. They followed a special pattern; however, a serious omen made a separate journey necessary in order to balance the extreme disorder anticipated for the (present) "latter days".

THE TRUE WHITE BROTHER

A Hopi of light complexion, now called the True Brother, left his people and travelled in the direction of the rising sun, taking with him a stone tablet which matches a similar tablet held by those who went on to meet Maasaw at a place called Oraibi. It was here that the present Hopi villages were established according to his instructions. The Hopi anticipated the arrival of a race of light-skinned people from the east, predicting many of their inventions, which would signal various stages of unfoldment of the pattern that the Hopi had studied since ancient times. It was clearly foreseen that the visitors in their cleverness might have lost sight of their original purpose, in which case they would become very dangerous. The Hopi were to watch for one who has not left the spiritual path and carries the actual stone tablet.

THE SWASTIKA AND THE SUN

Throughout the centuries, the Hopi have in their cere-monies recalled previous worlds, our emergence into the pre-sent world and our purpose in coming here. Periodically they have renewed their covenant with Maasaw to love the simple, humble way of life he laid out and to preserve the balance of Nature for the sake of all living things.

The knowledge of world events was handed down in secret lodges which kept watch as each stage unfolded. The elders looked especially for a series of three world-shaking events that would be accompanied by the appearance of certain symbols (crop formations matching the Hopi petroglyph sym-bols) describing the primordial forces that govern all life, from the sprouting of a seed to global events such as weather, earth-quakes, migrations and wars.

The gourd rattle is a key symbol, and its shaking during a ceremony means the stirring of life forces. On the rattle is drawn the ancient symbol of the swastika or *meha*, showing the spirals of force sprouting from a seed in four directions. This is surrounded by a ring of red fire, showing the encircling pene-tration of the warmth of the Sun, *tawa*, causing the seed to sprout and grow. The first two world-shaking events would involve forces portrayed by the swastika and the sun. Out of the violence and destruction of the first, the strongest elements would emerge with still greater force to produce the second event. When these actual symbols appeared, it would be a clear sign that this stage of the prophecy was being fulfilled.

THE GOURD FULL OF ASHES

Eventually, a "gourd full of ashes" would be invented, which if dropped from the sky would boil the oceans and burn the land, preventing anything from growing for many years.

This would be a signal for certain Hopi to reveal some of their teachings in order to warn the world that the third and final event would happen soon and that it could bring an end to all life unless people correct themselves in time. Hopi leaders now believe that the first two events were the first and second World Wars, and that the "gourd full of ashes" was the atomic bomb. After the obliteration of Hiroshima and Nagasaki, teachings formerly kept secret were compared, then released to the world. The details presented here are part of those teachings.

THE DAY OF PURIFICATION

The final stage, called the Day of Purification, is described as the hatching of a "mystery egg" in which the forces of *meha* and *tawa* unite with a third force symbolized by the colour red, culminating in either total rebirth or total annihilation—we don't know which, but the choice is still ours. War and natural catastrophe may be involved, but the degree of violence will be determined by the amount of disruption caused among the peoples of the world, and in the balance of Nature.

In this crisis, rich and poor will be forced to struggle as equals to survive. That it will be very violent is now taken for granted among the traditional Hopi societies, but even now we may still lessen its impact by correcting our treatment of Nature as well as of each other.

Ancient spiritually-based communities, such as the Hopi, must be preserved—and not forced to abandon their way of life or the resources they have vowed to protect.

THE FATE OF HUMANITY

Clearly, the Hopi have a key role to play in the survival of the human race, by virtue of their vital communion with the unseen forces that hold natural balance, and as an example of a practical alternative to suicidal man-made systems. They can thus be seen as a fulcrum of world events. The pattern is simple: "The whole world will shake, turn red and rise against those who are hindering the Hopi." The man-made systems now

219

destroying the Hopi culture are deeply involved in similar violations throughout the world and the devastating reversal predicated in the prophecies is merely part of the natural order. If those who thrive under that system and its money and its laws can prevent it from eliminating the Hopi Way, then many may survive the Day of Purification and enter a new age of peace. But if no-one is left to continue the Hopi Way, the hope for such an age is in vain.

The forces we must face are formidable, yet the only alternative is annihilation. The man-made system cannot be rectified by forcing others to do one's will, for that is the very crux of the problem. If people are to re-direct themselves and their leaders, the gulf between the two must be eliminated. To accomplish this, we can only rely on the energy of TRUTH itself. This approach, which is the foundation of the Hopi Way, is the greatest challenge a mortal can face. Few are likely to accept it. But once peace is established on this basis, and our *original* way of life is allowed to flourish, we will be able to use our inventive skills wisely to encourage rather than to threaten life, and benefit everyone, rather than enrich a few at the expense of others. Concern for all living things will far surpass personal concerns, bringing greater happiness and prosperity than could have been realised before. Then all living things shall enjoy lasting peace and harmony.

[Extracted from the *Global Purification Messenger*, journal of traditional Hopi Elders. The prophecies were condensed by Tom Tarbet and taken from the original given by DANAGYUMTEWA.]

A little later in the same chapter, the following item stopped me in my tracks. I think you'll know why!

George Washington, significantly a Freemason during the drawing up of the US Constitution (he denounced that cult during his last term of office), once had a memorable experience. He was visited by a beautiful female apparition, who showed him three dramatic scenes concerning the future of the

Republic. Finally, she said, "Son of the Republic, what you have seen is thus interpreted—three perils will come upon this Republic. The most fearful is the third, passing which, the whole world united shall never be able to prevail against her. Let every child of the Republic learn to live for his God, the land and the Union!"

Washington then said, "With these words the figure vanished. I started from my seat, and felt that I had been shown the birth, progress and destiny of the Republic of the United States: in her union she will have strength, in disunion her destruction."

These are words from Washington's own lips—and I respectfully suggest that every American, of whatever status, origin or creed, would do well to heed them. And not just Americans, but the rest of us, too. The Lady's final words apply to every nation, every person on Earth: how can we fail, if we respect the Mind that imagined the Universe, the planet we inhabit, and each other?!

The Lady again! Or rather, the Lady a few hundred years before *we* made her acquaintance! I am sure she has been appearing throughout history, in various guises, to every race. I am equally convinced that the luminous being who appeared to Bernadette Soubirous at Lourdes during the last century, and spoke to three young girls at Fatima, early this century, was not the Virgin Mary at all, but the One whom even *she* serves...]

COMPANIONS

Here are the titles of some of the books that have kept my friends and me company on our travels and adventures, and inspired us to seek further. Each one, in its own way, throws light on this crucial planetary moment:

ANCIENT WISDOM

[title]	[author]	[publisher]
THE INITIATION OF THE WORLD	Alder	Rider
INITIATION HUMAN & SOLAR	Bailey	Lucis Trust
A TREATISE ON WHITE MAGIC	Bailey	Lucis Trust
A SEARCH IN SECRET EGYPT	Brunton	Rider
INITIATION	Haich	Allen & Unwin
SECRET OF THE ANDES	Philip	Corgi
BHAGAVAD GITA	Prabhavananda	Mentor
SHAMBHALA OASIS OF LIGHT	Tomas	Sphere
AUTOBIOGRAPHY OF A YOGI	Yogananda	Rider

ASTROLOGY

ASTROLOGY—The Space Age Science	Goodavage	Prentice Hall
SUN SIGNS	Goodman	Pan
TWELVE SEATS AT THE ROUND TABLE	Matchett/ Trevelyan	Spearman

ASTRONOMY

THE NATURE OF THE UNIVERSE	Hoyle	Pelican

ATLANTIS

ATLANTIS TO THE LATTER DAYS	Stevens	Knights Templar
ATLANTIS FROM LEGEND	Tomas	Hale

TO DISCOVERY

AUTOBIOGRAPHY & BIOGRAPHY

JOURNEY TO IXTLAN	Castaneda	*Penguin*
A SEPARATE REALITY	Castaneda	*Penguin*
TALES OF POWER	Castaneda	*Simon & Schuster*
LENNON REMEMBERS	Lennon	*Penguin*
DOWN AND OUT IN PARIS AND LONDON	Orwell	*Penguin*

CLASSICS

THE PILGRIM'S PROGRESS	Bunyan	*Penguin*
THE SYMPOSIUM	Plato	*Penguin*
TIMAEUS	Plato	*Penguin*

CURRENT AFFAIRS

ARMAGEDDON	Vidal	*Grafton*
THE AQUARIAN CONSPIRACY	Ferguson	*RKP*
THE THIRD WAVE	Toffler	*Pan*
POWERSHIFT	Toffler	*Bantam*

FICTION

THE AVATARS	"A.E."	*Macmillan*
A GLASTONBURY ROMANCE	Powys	*Picador*
ILLUSIONS	Bach	*Dell*
THE LITTLE PRINCE	Saint-Exupery	*Puffin*

FUTURE

GLOBAL 2000—Report to the President		
CRITICAL PATH	Buckminster Fuller	*St Martins*
PROFILES OF THE FUTURE	Clarke	*Pan*
THE WIND OF CHANGE	Soskin	*Barton House*

HEALTH & HEALING

FIT FOR LIFE	Diamond	*Bantam*
FOOD FOR SPIRITUAL DEVELOPMENT	Kushi	*Order of the Universe*
HEALING SECRET OF THE AGES	Ponder	*Thomas*

HISTORY

THE ILLUMINED ONES	Cooke	*White Eagle*
THE LIGHT IN BRITAIN	Cooke	*White Eagle*
SUN-MEN OF THE AMERICAS	Cooke	*Spearman*
THE VIEW OVER ATLANTIS	Michell	*Abacus*
ETERNAL MAN	Pauwels/ Bergier	*Mayflower*
THE EPIC OF GILGAMESH	Sandars	*Penguin*
COSMIC MEMORY	Steiner	*Steiner*
THE DEATH OF MERLIN	Stein	*Floris*
THE KENNEDY CONSPIRACY	Summers	*Sphere*
WRITING ON THE GROUND	Tudor Pole	*Spearman*
EARTH IN UPHEAVAL	Velikovsky	*Abacus*
THE WILD SWANS	Yung Chang	*HarperCollins*

MYTH, LEGEND & REALITY

THE MISTS OF AVALON	Bradley	*Joseph*
THE SWORD AND THE FLAME	Christian	*Macmillan*
AVALON OF THE HEART	Fortune	*Aquarian*
TALIESIN	Lawhead	*Lion*
MERLIN	Lawhead	*Lion*
ARTHUR	Lawhead	*Lion*
THE ROMANCE OF KING ARTHUR	Malory	*Macmillan*
MERLIN AWAKES	Quiller	*Firebird*
MERLIN THE IMMORTAL	Quiller/Joseph	*Spirit of Celtia*
THE CRYSTAL CAVE	Stewart	*Coronet*
THE HOLLOW HILLS	Stewart	*Coronet*
THE WICKED DAY	Stewart	*Coronet*
SWORD AT SUNSET	Sutcliff	*Coronet*

THE ONCE AND FUTURE KING	White	*Fontana*
THE BOOK OF MERLIN	White	*Univ of Texas*
TALIESSIN THROUGH LOGRES	Williams	*Oxford*

OURSELVES

THE SHINING PATHS	Ashcroft-Nowicki	*Aquarian*
HIGHWAYS OF THE MIND	Ashcroft-Nowicki	*Aquarian*
THE PYRAMID AND THE GRAIL	Beckett	*Lailoken*
BOOK OF RUNES	Bloom	*Joseph*
THE ORACLE OF CHANGE— Consulting the I CHING	Douglas	*Penguin*
THE PATH OF THE SOUL	White Eagle	*White Eagle*

| Various THEOSOPHICAL Booklets: | | *TPH* |

KARMA
THE LAW OF SACRIFICE
LIVING TRUTH
MEDITATIONS
A STUDY OF KARMA, etc.

REFERENCE

| INNER DEVELOPMENT | Popenoe | *Penguin* |

REINCARNATION

THE WHEEL OF REBIRTH	Challoner	*TPH*
INITIATION	Haich	*Allen & Unwin*
OUR SON MOVES AMONG YOU	Long	*Bachman Turner*

RESEARCHING NATURE & MAN

| THE BOOK OF THE DAMNED | Fort | *Abacus* |
| NEW LANDS | Fort | *Sphere* |

225

THE EARTHQUAKE GENERATION	Goodman	*Turnstone*
MAN AND HIS SYMBOLS	Jung	*Picador*
THE DAWN OF MAGIC	Pauwels/ Bergier	*Gibbs*
SUPERNATURE	Watson	*Coronet*

SCIENCE FICTION

CHILDHOOD'S END	Clarke	*Pan*
TALES OF TEN WORLDS	Clarke	*Gollancz*
2001 A SPACE ODYSSEY	Clarke	*Arrow*
THE PUPPET MASTERS	Heinlein	*Pan*
DUNE MESSIAH	Herbert	*NEL*
STAR-BEGOTTEN	H G Wells	*Manor*

SPIRIT GUIDES

KNIGHTS OF THE SOLAR CROSS	Bender	*Regency*
THE FINDHORN GARDEN	Caddy	*Findhorn*
REGENTS OF THE SEVEN SPHERES	Challoner	*TPH*
THE GUIDE BOOK	Neate/H-A	*Gateway*
SETH SPEAKS Journey into the Self	Roberts	*Prentice Hall*
CONVERSATIONS WITH SETH	Watkins	*Prentice Hall*
MY DEAR ALEXIAS	WTP	*Spearman*
THE AWAKENING LETTERS	WTP	*Spearman*

SPIRIT WORLDS

LIFE IN THE WORLD UNSEEN	Borgia	*Corgi*
THE AWAKENING LETTERS	Lehmann/ Sandys	*Spearman*
A HANDBOOK OF ANGELS	Moolenburgh	*Daniel*
1 LOWLANDS OF HEAVEN	Vale Owen	*Greater World*
2 HIGHLANDS OF HEAVEN	Vale Owen	*Greater World*
3 MINISTRY OF HEAVEN	Vale Owen	*Greater World*
4 BATTALIONS OF HEAVEN	Vale Owen	*Greater World*
5 OUTLANDS OF HEAVEN	Vale Owen	*Greater World*

MICHAEL DEAN

THE THIRD MILLENNIUM

THE STARSEED TRANSMISSIONS	Carey	*HarperCollins*
STARSEEED, THE THIRD MILLENNIUM	Carey	*HarperCollins*
THE CELESTINE PROPHECY	Redfield	*Warner*

CURTAIN CALL

Thank you so much...

Kaye Challoner, Lady Cynthia Sandys, Rosamond Lehmann, Wellesley Tudor Pole, Roy Davis, Debbie Rice, Evelyn Winn, Peter Tuffnell, Steve Hillage, Peter Fuller, Tom Tarbet, Eileen Palmer and Sir George Trevelyan—for your important contributions.

Joyce Petschek, an experienced co-pilot/navigator, who patiently taught me to fly—and then fed me afterwards!

My Atlantean friends—for bringing the love, the simplicity and the majesty of H-A into my life.

Stuart Wilde of "The Mystic Trader", Box 1000, Taos, New Mexico 87571, and to Marshall Lever—for their generous permission to reprint "Merlin, Arthur and the Holy Grail" by "Old Chinese".

Maurice B. Cooke—for the inspiring message from Hilarion, taken from his series of Hilarion books, available from Marcus Books, PO Box 276, Lindsay, Ontario, Canada K9V 451.

Dolores Ashcroft-Nowicki—for allowing me to quote her inspiring description of the Grail Quest, which appears in *At the Table of the Grail*, [RKP], edited by John Matthews.

Anthony Roberts—whose mention of Merlin in *Atlantean Traditions in Ancient Britain* triggered my search for the Magician.

The Mail Diary, for kind permission to reprint "A

Bolt from Beyond", originally published in the *Daily Mail* on 30 January, 1990.

My love and thanks also go to:

Dear Alma—the magician who set all this in motion...

Sidney and Elsie—who shared their wisdom and commonsense so generously, and set my feet back on the path. I feel your presence even more strongly, now that you have gone on...

The lovely Merryn—a contemporary Morgan le Fay whose life of service and loyalty and love are an example to us all...

Julie—whose warmth, compassion, humour and generosity set standards that are dauntingly high...

Pete Carbines—whose wizardry with sound and imagery will soon be widely recognised...

Petey—for years of kinship, and your uncompromising wisdom...

John Prudhoe—brother, knight, whose knowledge and experience keep rising to the surface like water from an inexhaustible spring...

Zoë and Ted—who have a very special place in my mind and heart...

Peter Quiller—for starring in a most important chapter of my life; and, when that chapter ended, for challenging me to write this book—and for supplying *its* 46th chapter...!

Silver lady, golden hair—courageously working to re-establish the feminine energy in a world dominated—and largely ruined—by men...

Audrey—for loving and believing...

Ellen Easton—Earth mother and oracle—and her husband Tom, whose every day is spent in the service of others...

Gwynneth—the godmother *everyone* should have!

Simon—the valiant knight/warrior, forever riding into battle against infamy and injustice...

Kev—for just being you...

Snow White [Michelle]—for showing me that there *is* solid gold to be found beneath the sidewalks of Tinsel Town; and for holding my hand on the Boulevard of Dreams...

Joshua and Aly—for bringing the future into the present...

His Excellency the Honorable Juan ["JC"] Brown, Ambassador and Plenipotentiary from the Court of Waxmania—for bringing some much-needed light, laughter and love to the grime and madness of Hollywood Boulevard...

Karen—for providing a haven, a second family and yet more laughter in the Badlands of California...

Jerry—brother, knight, warrior, friend; wellspring of Texas wisdom and perception...

James Bell, a true Aquarian and galactic man—

whose effortless grasp of universal principles and energies is matched by an outrageous sense of humour. Your friendship has been more precious than diamonds...

Tony—for years and years of insight and integrity—and for becoming the most extraordinary creative partner, compass and guide...

Ava, the eternal woman—who has been such a rich source of inspiration. And still is, and always will be...

And, of course, the Guardians—for every reason imaginable.

Index

Acapulco, 44
Albion, Giant, 14
Alcania, 125
alchemists, 52, 102
Alder, Vera Stanley, 195
Alexander of Tunis, Field
  Marshall the Earth, 58
Alma [see Cogan]
Ambrosius, 121
American Indians, 40, 86, 97
Ancient Wisdom, 10, 140, 169
Andrews, tony, 12, 13, 18, 20, 26,
  27, 86, 87
Angels, 3, 33–35, 153
Apache, the, 215
Anrias, David, 33
Aquitaine, 121
Archangel Michael, 7, 96, 182,
  204
Archmage [see Merlin]
Ark of the Covenant, 165
Armageddon, 70
Arthur, King [see King Arthur]
Ar-tor [see King Arthur]
Ashcroft-Nowicki, Dolores,
  161–163
astrological signs [see Zodiac]
At The Table of The Grail, 161
Atlantean Tradition in Ancient
  Britain, 3, 14
Atlanteans, 38, 79, 80
Atlantis, 3, 14, 68, 169
Auchinleck, Field Marshal Sir
  Claude, 58
Audley End, 91, 92
Audrey Charlton, 42, 186, 187
Australian abriginals, 40

Ava [see Gardner, Ava]
Avalon, Return To, 120–127
Avatars, 117, 118
Avignon, Popes of, 95

Bacchanalia, 65
Bacchus, 65
Bailey, Alice, 58
Balaban, Bob, 91
Bardot, Brigitte, 189
Battle For The Earth, 70, 72, 204
Bedevere, Sir, 166
Bell, James, 4–6, 106, 176, 187,
  190
Bernadette Soubirous, 221
Blake, William, 14
Blithe Spirit, 33
Bloy, Colin, 95
Bradley, Marion, 131
Brooks, Louise, 180
Bruckner, Anton, 39
Buckingham Palace, 55
Buddha, 139, 184
Bush, President George, 190, 191

Camelot, 137–139, 214
Canterbury Cathedral, 92
Carbines, Peter, 17, 72, 73
Cassiopeia, 54, 55, 207
Catch The Lightning, 17, 42, 45,
  78–82, 190
Cathars, 95
Chaldeans, 122
Chalice Hill, Glastonbury, 26
Chalice Well, Glastonbury, 26
Challoner, Kaye, 33
Charles, Prince [see Prince of

Wales]
Chartres Cathedral, 97
Christ, 58, 96, 102, 122, 169
Christian, Catherine, 131
Christine [*Mrs. Peter Joseph*], 41,
    42, 65,66
Church Militant, 92–94
Churchill, Sir Winston, 39, 84,
    206, 213
Circle of Light, the, 77–82, 92
Circle of Magicians, the, 132,
    133, 134, 140, 195
Circle of Power, the, 91–94, 96
Circlet, gold, 182–184
City of Revelation, 3, 77
Close Encounters of The Third
    Kind, 4, 91, 115
Cogan, Alma, 187
Confucius, 139
Constitution of Great Britain,
    214
Constitution of the USA, 220
corn circles, 102
Cornwall, 86, 122, 132
Cornwall, Duchess of, 132
Coward, Noël,
creative intelligence, 54, 58, 60,
    68, 142, 159
Creator, the, *passim*
Cromwell, Oliver, 92
Cross, 183
Cross of Illumination, 117, 118
Crown [*see Hollows of the Grail*]
Crown Jewels, the, 213
crystal cave, 113
crystals, 54, 119, 138
Cukor, George, 44
Cup [*see Hollows of the Grail*]

Daily Mail, 189
Dark Ages, 93

Davis, Royu, 110, 111
Dean, Michael, *passim*
Dee, Dr. John, 14
Dee, Simon, 13, 77, 83
deGaulle, Charles, 98
Devereux, Bill and Elsie, 78
Diane, Princess [*see Princess of
    Wales*]
Dionysus, 139
Draco, 54, 55, 100, 105, 207
dreams, 41, 67, 74, 119, 137,
    138, 198
Donaldson, Robert, 22
Dweller at the Threshold, 171

Earth, 16, 19, 37, 47, 51, 58, 68,
    71, 74, 75, 83, 84, 105, 109,
    115, 117–119, 123–5, 134, 137,
    140, 141, 144, 153–155, 164,
    172, 174, 221
Egypt, 110, 115, 122, 134
Elaine, 163, 166, 167
Elgar, Sir Edward, 39, 80
Elizabeth, Empress of Austria, 44
ET, The Extraterrestrial, 4
European Economic Community,
    213
Excalibur, 15, 85, 95, 96, 133,
    139, 167, 182, 184

Fantasia, 88
Fatima, 221
Finnish Angel, the, 35
Fuller, Simon Peter, 215–221

G7 Summit, 190, 191
Galahad, Sir, 166, 173, 174
Garbo, Greta, 188
Gardner, Ava, 42–45, 179–181,
    186–191, 194, 201, 202
Gawain, Sir, 166, 171, 174

233

gemstones, 179
Geronimo, 98
Glastonbury, 12, 26–28, 140
A Glastonbury Romance, 161
Glastonbury Tor, 26, 27, 77, 79, 87
Glastonbury Zodiac, 14, 141
Gloucestershire, 77, 100
Goddess, 188
Golden Valley, 89, 106
Gorbachev, President Mikhail, 190, 191
Gort, Field Marshall Viscount, 58
Grail, the, 80, 103, 135, 137–139, 142, 149, 161, 165–171, 173, 174, 183
Grail Stone of the Albigenses, 95
Grail Table, 173
Great Bear [see Ursa Major]
Great Britain, 10, 11, 26–28, 39, 55, 68, 80, 92, 96, 97, 100, 121, 132, 134, 165, 213, 214
Great Invocation, the, 84
Great Pyramid, 134
Greece, 139
Guardian, the, 71–75
guardian rock, the, 79, 81, 84, 89, 107, 111
Guardians, the, 54, 65–68, 96, 137, 182, 207–209, 211
Guarding Merlin's Enclosure, 165–174
Guinevere [see Queen Guinevere]

H-A [see Helio-Arcanophus]
Hall of the Akashic Record, 120
Hallows of Great Britain, 213, 214
Hallows of the Grail: 168, 169
the Cup, 54, 105, 168
The Lance, 168

the Sword, 102, 105, 113, 114, 168, 169, 182, 184
the Scabbard, Dish or Stone, 169
the Nails, 169
the Crown, 169
Hammerstein, Oscar, 98
A Handbook Of Angels, 3, 34, 35
Hartland Abbey, 64
"heathen," 93
Hector, Sir, 166, 167
Helio-Arcanophus, 10, 38, 85, 95
Hemingway, Ernest, 181
Henry VI, 103
Herefordshire, 77, 103
"heresy," 93
"heretic," 93
Hilarion, 153, 154
Hillage, Steve, 149
Hitler, Adolf, 39, 206
Hoddle, Glenn, 207
Hollywood, 44, 45, 180, 189
homometry, 146
Holst, Gustav, 30
Holy Grail [see Grail]
Holy Lady [see the Lady]
Hopi, the, 215–220
Hopkins, Matthew, 92
Horus, 117–119

India, 115
Initiation, Human And Solar, 58
Initiations, 57, 108–128
Instant Karma, 158
Iona, 107
Isle of Wight, 96
Ivinghoe Beacon, 55

James Bell [see Bell]
Janus, 162
Johnson, "Magic," 207

Jubilee, HM the Queen's, 46
Julie, "the divine" [see Peasgood]

Karma, 46–49, 51
Kean, Betty, 188
A Key Unto The Language of
    America, 97
King, the, 54, 58, 65, 67, 68, 96,
    100, 101, 114, 132, 142, 159,
    182, 184, 207–209, 211
King Arthur, 7, 78, 96, 103,
    121–126, 131–133, 135,
    137–139, 163, 165–169, 172,
    213
King William II, 91
Kings, 68, 78, 151, 213
Kneff, Hildegard, 180
Knights and Ladies, 100, 101,
    147–156
Knights of the Cross, 128
Knights of the Round Table, 100,
    101, 126, 131, 165–174
Knights of the Round Table, 181

Lady, the, 54, 61, 62, 64, 67, 80,
    96, 114, 142, 159, 183, 184,
    186, 188, 207–209, 211, 221
Lady of the Lake [see Vivien]
Lance [see Hallows of the Grail]
Lancelot, Sir, 133, 139, 163, 166,
    171, 172, 174
Lao-Tse, 139
Layla, 12, 13
Lehmann, Rosamond, 84
Lennon, John, 158, 176
Lever, Marshall, 137–139
Links With Space, 17–20, 22
Wanwit Major, 87, 88
Lloyd George, David, 213
Los Angels Olympics, 46
Lot, King of Lothian, 17

Lourdes, 221
Love, Adrian, 22
love/wisdom, 40, 54, 58, 60, 68,
    142
Lower Saxony, 121

Maclaine, Shirley, 98, 180
magic, 145, 206–212
Mage [see Merlin]
Magician [see Merlin]
Magna Carta, 213
Mahler, Gustav, 39,
Malory, Sir Thomas, 131, 181
Malvern Hills, 77–82, 96, 100,
    103, 110
"Manittoo!", 97
Manitou—The Sacred Landscape
    of New England's Native
    Civilization, 97
Mary Magdalene, 62
Master of Ceremonies, the, 65-
    –67, 96, 135, 159, 207–209
matter, 78, 20, 145, 147, 148
Matthews, John and Caitlin, 161
Maya, the, 215
medicine of the plains, 97
Meeres, Nicolette, 29

Merlin:
    makes an entrance, 5, 6
    "Who is Merlin?," 7
    the reappearance of, 10
    "Merlin will awake," 10
    a prophecy fulfilled, 10
    the Archange, 11
    "Merlin's Secret," 14
    Merlin speaks, 16
    as co-author, 17
    selects a channel, 23
    a voice like thunder, 24
    guide, tutor and friend, 26

a gift, 27, 29
"hidden powers," 38–44
answers a letter, 49–51
as one of the Guardians, *passim*
does a voice-over, 73
gives a map reference, 91
the master of words, 98, 99
a personal initiation, 112–114
5th century flashback, 132–135
"He came through crystal,"
　138
"Merlin is your higher self,"
　139
"Who on Earth is Merlin?,"
　140
defines "magic," 145, 207
a vision of the future, 147, 148,
　177, 178
Exit the Wizard, 159, 160
as personal tutor, 161
a parting gift, 176–178
the crowning, 182–184
Merlin engine, 27
Merlin hawk, 26
Merlin's Enclosure, 11
Merlinus Albonis [*see Merlin*]
Merryn Jose, 187
Michael Saint [*see Archangel
　Michael*]
Michell, John, 3, 77
Mitchell, RJ, 27
Moolenburgh, Dr. HC, 3, 34
Mordred, 167, 168
Morgan Le Fay, 62, 133, 139,
　167, 191
Morgause, 167, 168
Morte d'Arthur, 181
Mr. Universe, 180
Muses, 66
music, 8, 9, 11, 18, 27, 28, 38,
　39, 65, 66, 72, 80, 101, 107,

142, 149, 184, 190, 200
mystery schools, 110, 161

Navajo, the, 215
Nelson, Horatio, 213
Nicolette [*see Meeres*]
North Pole, 05
Norwich Cathedral, 92

O'Casey, Sean, 213
"Old Chinese," 137–139
'Omega point [year 2013], 215
Onassis, Aristotle, 189
"Operation Excalibur," 86, 95, 96
O'Rahilly, Ronan, 28
Orion, 65, 207
Oval Office, 191–194
Oxford, 92–187

Pain, Thomas, 147
Palmer, Eileen, 203, 204
Park Wood, 12–14
Path to the Grail, the, 161–163
Peasgood, Julie, 41
Percival, Sir, 166, 169–171, 174
Petey [*see Tuffriell*]
Pharaohs, 68, 118
Picasso, Pablo, 39
The Planets Suite, 80
Pole star, 105, 106
Portobello Road, 42, 87
Posey, Edward, 106
Powys, John Cowper, 161
Prince of Wales, 55
Princess of Wales, 98
Prudhoe, John, 10, 30, 31, 91,
　92, 106, 120–127
Pythagoras, 139

Queen Elizabeth I, 14, 213

Queen Elizabeth II, 68, 69, 213
Queen Guinevere, 44, 133, 139, 167
Queens and Empresses, 68, 135, 213
Quest for the Holy Grail, 103, 135, 136–139, 161, 181
Quiller, Peter, 22–24, 27, 36, 54 ,55, 65, 72, 73, 86, 95, 96, 100, 101, 105–107, 131–136, 150, 182, 206–212

Radio Caroline, 28
Ragged Stone Hill, 78–82, 84, 88, 89, 91, 95, 106, 110, 111
Raleigh, Sir Walter, 213
rays, 58
Regents of the Seven Spheres, 33
Regent's Park, 30, 31, 71
reincarnation, 47, 49, 50, 51
Rennes-le-Château, 95, 102
Rice, Debbie, II, 165–175
Robert the Bruce, 213
Roberts, Anthony, 3, 14
Roerich, Nikolai, 35
Round Table, the, 57, 123, 131, 162, 163
Royce, Sir Henry, 27
Rutherford, Dame Margaret, 33

Saffron Walden, 91, 96
Saint Angel of Light [see Archangel Michael]
Saint George, 96
Saint Michael [see Archangel Michael]
Sandys, Lady Cynthia, 84
Saturnalia, 65
Scott, Cyril, 33
Scott, Si Walter, 213
Sellers, Peter, 189

Sergeant Pepper, 61
Shakespeare, William, 103, 213
Shostakovitch, Dimitri, 39
"siege perilous, the," 173
The Sign of the Dove, 102, 103
Silbury Hill, 86, 87
Silver, 12, 13, 26, 27
Sioux, the, 215
Slim, Field Marshall Viscount, 58
solar system, 20, 117
Sorcerer's Apprentice, The, 88
Soskin, Julie, 195–199
sound, 38, 100, 112, 141, 178, 198, 200
Soviet Union, 70, 191
Spielberg, Steven, 115
Spitfire, 26, 27
Stalin, Josef, 39
Sandcumbe, Tony, 78, 186, 187
Starship Earth, 16, 19, 164
Steinbeck, John, 181
Stewart, Mary, 131
Stonehenge, 77, 134
Sun, 58, 115–118, 125, 195, 218
swastika, the, 218
Sword [see Hollows of the Grail]

Tara, 214
Tchaikovsky, Peter, 39
technology, 4, 145, 146, 155, 161, 177, 217
"There is no death," 74
Thomas, Dylan, 213
Thorburn, Jacqueline [Murry Hope], 79, 80
Thoth, 203
Tibet, 115
Tintagel Castle, 132
Trevelyan, Sir George, 7, 8
Tudor Pole, Wellesley, 84, 85, 141
Tuffnell, Peter [Petey], 26, 29, 33,

35, 58, 84, 149, 161

United Kingdom, 39, 214
United States of America, 39, 87, 97, 98, 192, 221
Universal Declaration of Human Rights, 144
Universe, the, *passim*
Ursa Major ["The Plough" or "The Great Bear"], 54, 55, 159, 207
Utopia, 196

Van Buren, Elizabeth, 102, 103
Vaughan Williams, Ralph, 80
VE Day, 46
Vega, 106
Venus, 102
Venus, Goddess of Love, 44
The View Over Atlantis, 3, 77
Virgin Mary, 221
Vivien, Lady of the Lake, 167
voice, 39, 40

Wagner, Richard, 39
Wales, 87, 88, 123
Wand [*see Hollows of the Grail*]
Washington, George, 220, 221

Warell, Field Marshall Lord, 58
The Wheel of Rebirth, 33
The White Brotherhood, 117
White Leafe Oak, 78, 79, 88, 95
White, TH, 131
Wilderness, 22
will, 54, 58, 60, 68, 142
William II [*see King William II*]
The Wind of Change, 195–199, 204
Windsor Great Park, 17
Windsor, House of, 213
Winn, Evelyn, 112–114
Wizard [*see Merlin*]
the Wizard of Oz, 159
Worcestershire, 77, 95
Worcestershire Beacon, 81
World War I, 34, 35, 219
World War II, 34, 35, 206, 219
Wren, Sir Christopher, 213

Yeats, William Butler, 213
York, 96

Zodiac, the, 57, 171, 172, 173, 209
Zoroaster, 139